MARYLAND REAL ESTATE COMMISSION

RESPONSIBLE FOR IMPLEMENTATION OF LICENSING LAWS AND PROTECTING THE PUBLIC IN REAL ESTATE RELATED MATTERS

APPOINTED BY GOVERNOR WITH
ADVICE & CONSENT OF STATE SENATE

ADVICE OF SECRETARY OF LICENSING
& REGULATION

CURRENTLY 9 MEMBERS
4 YEAR TERMS BEGINNING
JUNE 1ST (STAGGERED)

5 PROFESSIONAL MEMBERS *(LICENSED)*	4 CONSUMER MEMBERS *(UNLICENSED)*

SPECIFIC AREA	10 YRS. LICENSED	5 YRS. RESIDENT	AT LARGE	NO REAL ESTATE FOR 1 YEAR

CHAIRPERSON *(ONE OF THE COMMISSIONERS)*	EXECUTIVE DIRECTOR *(UNLICENSED/NOT COMM.)*

1 YEAR TERM	APPOINTED BY SEC. FROM 3 NOMINEES OF THE COMM

SERVES AT PLEASURE OF
THE SECRETARY

PAID FROM STATE BUDGET

CHAIRPERSON AND EXECUTIVE DIRECTOR
ARE COVERED BY A BOND

THE MEMBERS OF THE REAL ESTATE COMMISSION APPOINTED BY THE GOVERNOR CAN ALSO BE REMOVED FROM THE COMMISSION BY THE GOVERNOR.

11/96

Maryland
Real Estate:
Practice & Law

NINTH EDITION

H. WARREN CRAWFORD
DONALD A. WHITE

**Real Estate
Education Company**®
a division of Dearborn Financial Publishing, Inc.

Executive Editor: Diana Faulhaber
Art Manager: Lucy Jenkins
Editorial Assistant: Kelley Prosser

Published by Real Estate Education Company ®,
a division of Dearborn Financial Publishing, Inc.®
155 North Wacker Drive
Chicago, IL 60606-1719
(312) 836-4400
http://www.real-estate-ed.com

Library of Congress Cataloging-in-Publication Data

White, Donald Allen, 1931-
    Maryland real estate : practice & law / Donald A. White,
H. Warren Crawford. — 9th ed.
        p.   cm.
    Rev. ed. of Maryland supplement for Modern real estate practice.
8th ed. / H. Warren Crawford, Donald A. White.
    Includes index.
    ISBN 0-7931-3181-2
    1. Real estate business—Law and legislation—Maryland.
2. Vendors and purchasers—Maryland. 3. Real property—Maryland.
I. Crawford, H. Warren. II. White, Donald A. Maryland supplement
    for Modern real estate practice. III. Title.
KF2042.R4G34 1996 Maryland
346.75204'37—dc21   98-33295
                                                              CIP

Contents

Preface

As a student entering a real estate course you face exciting challenges. You must learn a large body of theory and then apply it to practice. Make the most of your classroom opportunities. You will want to know legal principles and real estate theory so well that when you get your license you will be able to "do the right thing" almost automatically. If you fail to understand and appreciate law and theory, you can suffer devastating financial and legal consequences. If you build your educational foundation in real estate well, you will be able to make the money you want and keep the money you make.

The purpose of this volume is to present laws and operating procedures for real estate in the State of Maryland. It builds on basic information presented in the text, *Modern Real Estate Practice,* by Galaty, Allaway and Kyle. Every effort has been made to avoid duplicating information presented in *Modern Real Estate Practice.* Therefore, you should study each subject area in the basic text and then refer to the same subject area in this book. Some chapters in the basic text have no related chapter in this volume because the subject matter does not involve laws or practices that vary significantly from state to state. While care has been exercised in providing information pertaining to the laws governing the practice of real estate in Maryland, **the reader is urged to consult with legal counsel regarding any statutory enactment and should not rely solely on this publication as legal authority for compliance with any statute.**

Following most chapters are review questions. They can provide both an evaluative tool and a learning technique. As you finish each chapter, and before you go on to the next, be certain that you are able to answer **and understand** each question presented. An answer key for all of the tests is included at the end of the book.

Throughout your real estate course, you'll be studying and taking tests in preparation for the Maryland Real Estate Examination. That examination is prepared and administered for the State Real Estate Commission by an independent testing service, Psychological Services, Inc. (PSI), of Glendale, California. *Maryland Real Estate: Practice and Law* has been designed to familiarize you with the kinds of items you'll find on that examination. The questions at the end of each chapter are prepared in a format similar to those in the licensing examination.

The authors appreciate the constructive suggestions on the updating and revision of this text provided by Dr. Darlene Mallick. We also extend our thanks to Kelley Prosser, Editorial Assistant at Real Estate Education Company, who diligently shepherded this work to completion.

Maryland Real Estate: Practice & Law, Ninth Edition, is written by H. Warren "Buck" Crawford, Esq., of Ocean City, Maryland, and Donald A.. White, GRI®, DREI, of Bowie, Maryland.

Mr. Crawford maintains the law firm formerly known as Crawford & Crawford, a general law practice in Ocean City, Maryland. He is also president of St. Martins Real Estate Company, REALTORS®. He has been licensed to practice real estate in Maryland since 1948. He holds a *Juris Doctor* from the University of Baltimore.

A past president of the Maryland Association of REALTORS® and of the Ocean City Board of REALTORS®, Mr Crawford was also a national director of the National Association of REALTORS®, as well as a founder and Dean of the REALTORS® Institute of Maryland. Mr. Crawford has taught real estate courses at Ocean City College, the University of Baltimore and the REALTORS® Institute of Maryland.

Mr. White has been a Maryland real estate licensee since 1967, holding an associate broker license since 1972. He earned degrees from Hofstra University, Southern Baptist Theological Seminary, and Central Michigan University. He has taught real estate pre-licensing and other business subjects at Prince George's Community College since 1972. He served several terms as Chair of the Education Committee of the Prince George's Association of REALTORS®. He also served as President of the Maryland Real Estate Educators Association, and is presently a member of the Educational Advisory Committee to the Education Committee of the Maryland Real Estate Commission.

Mr. White holds the DREI designation from the Real Estate Educators Association. He has taught frequently in REALTOR® continuing education seminars. He also was the principal author of **Questions and Answers on Maryland Real Estate** and co-author, with Maurice Boren, of the **Study Guide to Maryland Real Estate License Examinations.**

The authors welcome suggestions for improving this volume and ask that they be sent to the publisher and labeled "for Maryland Real Estate: Practice & Law."

Maryland Real Estate License Law and Related Regulations

OVERVIEW

The Maryland Real Estate Brokers Act, the subject of much of this chapter, became effective in its original form June 1, 1939. Since then there have been frequent revisions. All the work of real estate licensees is affected by this statute.

Real estate brokerage is governed both by statutory law and administrative law. Title 17, Sections 17-101 through 17-702 of the Business Occupations and Professions Article, of the Annotated Code of Maryland, the "Maryland Real Estate Brokers Act," was enacted by the General Assembly. Therefore, it is referred to as *legislative (statutory)* law. This volume refers to this statute as the "Brokers Act." The Maryland Real Estate Commission and the Department of Licensing and Regulation make and enforce regulations to implement the statute. These regulations are *administrative* law.

A copy of the Brokers Act, in a booklet that also contains relevant portions of the regulations, is available upon request from the Commission, 501 St. Paul Place, 8th Floor South, Baltimore, MD 21202-2272, or from a local Board or Association of REALTORS®. Many college and public libraries may have law changes passed since the last publication of the booklet. Look for it in the Legal Reference section. The *Maryland Register,* a bi-weekly publication, reports both proposed and finalized changes in regulations and announces regular monthly Commission meetings.

The State Government Legislative Reference service, (301) 858-3810, can provide copies of proposed new or changed statutes. Copies of pending legislation can also be found and downloaded from the web page of the Maryland General Assembly on the Internet at *http://mlis.state.md.us/*. There click "Bill Information and Status"; then, under "Bill Indexes," click "One or Two Subjects."

The statutes and regulations contained in this volume are those in force at the time of its publication, including changes passed to take effect Jan. 1, 1999. An updated law booklet that includes recent changes will be distributed by the Commission in 1999.

DEFINITIONS OF TERMS

As used in the statute, certain words have special definitions unless the context requires otherwise. For example, **a real**

estate broker is defined as an individual who provides **real estate brokerage services**. These services are defined as any of the following activities:

- For consideration and for another person: selling, buying, exchanging or leasing any real estate, or collecting rent for the use of any real estate
- For consideration assisting another person to locate or obtain for purchase or lease any residential real estate
- Engaging in a business of regularly buying and selling real estate or leases or options on real estate
- Engaging in a business that promotes the sale of real estate through a listing in a publication issued primarily for that purpose
- Engaging in the business of subdividing land and selling the subdivided lots
- For consideration serving as a consultant for any of the activities in this list

Although the law defines **persons** as "individuals, receivers, trustees, guardians, personal representatives, fiduciaries or representatives of any kind and any partnership, firm, association or other entity," only individuals may hold licenses. Licenses are also issued that show trade names under which licensed individuals deliver brokerage services. The Commission issues three levels of **license**: broker, associate broker and salesperson. In the statute and in this volume, *Commission* refers to the State Real Estate Commission. When the term *licensed* is used, it refers to the status of an individual licensed by the Commission.

Individuals who **affiliate** with brokers enter into employment or other contractual relationships with them. Throughout this volume, the term *affiliate*, used as a noun, will refer to licensed **associate brokers and licensed salespersons. Associate brokers** are individuals who have met educational and testing requirements for becoming real estate brokers but whose licenses authorize them only to provide real estate brokerage services *on behalf of* brokers with whom they are affiliated; their duties and authority are no greater than those of salespersons. **Salespersons** are individuals who aid the brokers with whom they are affiliated in providing real estate brokerage services.

Real estate is defined as an interest in real property anywhere. It includes interests in condominiums, time-share estates, and time-share licenses, as those terms are defined in the *Real Property Article*. In the statute the term **includes** means "includes but is not limited to."

In the Brokers Act, the term **state** refers to any state in the United States, its territories, possessions or the District of Columbia. In this volume when **State** is capitalized, it refers to the State of Maryland. In the law, the **Department** refers to the Department of Labor, Licensing and Regulation in which the Commission is found. The **Secretary** refers to the Secretary of Labor, Licensing and Regulation, the executive officer of The Department.

SCOPE OF THE BROKERS ACT

Certain persons who perform real estate activities are not governed by the Brokers Act. They are

- persons acting under a judgment or order of a court;
- public officers performing the duties of office;
- persons engaging in a single transaction that involves the sale or lease of any real estate if they are acting under a power of attorney executed by the owner of the real estate;
- licensed auctioneers selling any real estate at public auction;
- owners or lessors of any real estate, unless the primary business of the owner or lessor is providing real estate brokerage services; and
- persons acting as receivers, trustees, personal representatives or guardians.

In contrast, certain other persons, when performing acts of real estate brokerage, must conform to the relevant requirements of the Brokers Act although they need not hold real estate licenses. They are

- financial institutions in the leasing or selling of property they have acquired through foreclosure or by receiving a deed or an assignment in lieu of foreclosure;
- lawyers not regularly engaged in the business of providing real estate services and who do not communicate to the public that they are in such business;
- home builders in the rental or initial sale of homes they have constructed;
- agents of a licensed real estate broker or of an owner of real estate while managing or leasing that real estate for that broker or owner;
- persons who negotiate the sale, lease or transfer of businesses when the sale does not include any interest in real property other than the lease

for the property where the business operates; and
- owners who subdivide and sell not more than six lots of their own unimproved property in a calendar year. If they or their family have owned the property ten years or more, there is generally no limit on the number they may sell.

A real estate licensee typically is not required to obtain an additional license as a trailer dealer to sell mobile homes that will ultimately be used in fixed locations as residences. Neither is a real estate license required for selling cemetery plots. In some counties, a *bona fide* charitable organization can conduct a raffle for its exclusive benefit when the prize to be awarded is real property to which the organization holds title or has the ability to convey title. An organization may not conduct more than two raffles of real property in any calendar year. The State's Attorney of the county in which a raffle is contemplated should be consulted.

REAL ESTATE COMMISSION

The Real Estate Commission is one of several commissions within the Department of Labor, Licensing and Regulation. It consists of nine members, five of whom are licensees chosen, one each, from the Eastern Shore, Baltimore Metropolitan Area, Baltimore City, Southern Maryland and Western Maryland. They must have held Maryland real estate licenses at least ten years, and have resided in the areas from which they are appointed for at least five years, both immediately prior to their appointment. Four others are consumer members who may not have had an ownership interest in or received compensation from an entity regulated by the

Commission in the year just before their appointment. Members are appointed by the Governor with the advice of the Secretary and advice and consent of the Senate. Membership terms, which are staggered to ensure continuity, begin on June 1 and end four years later, either with reappointment or upon the appointment of a qualified replacement. Members may be removed before the end of their terms by the Governor in cases of incompetence or misconduct.

Each year members of the Commission elect a chairperson to preside at its meetings. This officer is covered by a surety bond. The Commission holds a public meeting each month with a majority of the members constituting a quorum. With ten days' advance written notice a member of the public may address the Commission. It has adopted bylaws for the conduct of its meetings and regulations for the conduct of hearings and for issuance of licensing applications. The Commission's Executive Director, who is appointed by and serves at the pleasure of the Secretary, is not one of its members and is different from its Chairperson. The Executive Director, a State Employee, directs the day-to-day operations of the Commission and its employed staff between monthly meetings.

Both Covered by a Bond

DUTIES AND POWERS OF THE COMMISSION

The Commission adopts, maintains, and enforces a Code of Ethics and General Regulations that set forth standards of conduct for all individuals licensed under the Act. The Code of Ethics and the General Regulations are part of COMAR – the Code of Maryland Regulations. At least every two years the Commission is required to provide a copy of its Code of

Ethics and its Regulations to every licensee and, upon request, to any person at any time. Commission Regulations are reflected in this volume.

The Commission has many other powers and duties. It administers and enforces the provisions of the Brokers Act by investigating complaints about licensee behavior, holding hearings, administering oaths, issuing subpoenas for the attendance of witnesses or for the production of evidence, and taking depositions. In certain special circumstances it is authorized to seek injunctions. The Commission must conduct an investigation relating to any complaint received in writing, under oath, alleging that an unauthorized person has provided real estate brokerage services. On request of any person and payment of the required fee, it will certify the licensing status and qualifications of any person who is the subject of the request. It has the power and duty to approve the content of educational courses for licensing and for continuing education. The Commission pays all money it collects under this Act into the General Fund of the State. It submits an annual report of its activities to the Secretary. **Hearing boards,** appointed by the Commission from among its own membership, have three members, at least one of whom must be a consumer member and one a **professional member** (licensee). The Commission administers a **Guaranty Fund** to reimburse members of the public as much as $25,000 for actual losses caused by certain misdeeds of licensees and certain of their employees.

LICENSING

In general, individuals must be licensed by the Commission as real estate brokers, or as associate brokers or salespersons affiliated with and working under licensed brokers, before providing real estate brokerage services in the State.

Brokers

To qualify for the real estate broker license, applicants must be of good character and reputation, at least 18 years old, have completed a 135-hour course in real estate approved by the Commission for real estate brokers, have been licensed as real estate salespersons actively and lawfully for at least three years and have passed the broker pre-license examination. If applicants are qualified to practice law in the State, the Commission waives the education and experience requirements. Broker education requirements are not interchangeable with those for salespersons. An individual who has actively and regularly engaged in real estate practice as a licensed real estate broker in another state for at least three of the five years immediately preceding submission of application is considered to have satisfied the educational requirements.

Associate Brokers

To qualify for associate real estate broker licenses, applicants must meet the basic requirements for real estate broker license described above and also obtain from a licensed real estate broker a commitment providing that they shall become affiliated with that real estate broker when they become licensed.

Salespersons

To qualify for active salesperson licenses, applicants must be of good character and reputation, be at least 18 years of age, successfully complete a basic 60-hour course in real estate approved by the

Commission, pass the required examination and obtain from a licensed real estate broker a commitment providing that they shall become affiliated with that broker as a real estate salesperson when licensed. In 1998, the General Assembly reduced the requirement for salesperson education from 90 to 60 hours, effective October 1 of that year. The law requires that the pre-license course include instruction in human relations and fair housing.

GENERAL RULES

All applicants must complete education requirements before taking exams. After passing both parts of each exam, they must apply for licensure within one year or be subject to re-examination. They must apply on-line over the Internet—or on the Commission's paper application forms—and pay the required fees as shown in Figure 1. All applicants who are not residents of this State must submit to the Commission their **irrevocable consent**. This consent allows the licensee to be served with official documents without the server's having to travel to a foreign (out-of-state) jurisdiction to present them. All applicants are required to submit any additional documentation that the Commission requires in order to determine their professional competence or good character and reputation. Broker applicants must also submit or pay for a credit report. *Salesperson doesn't need credit repo*

The Commission may waive any requirement for individual licenses for applicants who hold comparable or equivalent licenses granted by another state if those applicants pay the required application fees, meet the relevant requirements and submit certified copies of their licenses from the other states. If applicants are seeking broker licenses based on their comparable licenses in another state, they must provide adequate evidence of actively maintaining brokerage offices there.

All license certificates and pocket cards that the Commission issues to affiliates show the names of the licensed real estate brokers with whom they are affiliated, as those names appear on their brokers' licenses. Note that, although issued to licensees, the certificates are sent to and maintained in the brokerage office where they work.

Generally, licenses are granted for a two-year term from their date of issuance. Until 1998, licenses expired on either March 1, for brokers or April 30, for affiliates. In 1998, those renewing their licenses were given terms ranging, by days, from 6 to 30 months. At the next renewal, every applicant will receive a two-year term. All *initial* licenses granted in 1998 were for terms of two years from their dates of issuance. Affiliates may apply to the Commission to transfer their affiliation from one broker to another after obtaining from the new broker a commitment stating that, on cancellation of the current affiliation and issuance of new license certificates and pocket cards, they will become affiliated with the new broker. They shall also submit a statement of terminated relationship either from their former brokers or from themselves with their transfer applications.

Real estate brokers' licenses authorize them to provide real estate brokerage services to the public. Associate brokers' and salespersons' licenses, however, authorize those individuals to provide such services only on behalf of the licensed real estate brokers with whom they are affiliated, and never on their own behalf or on behalf of brokers with whom they are not affiliated.

EXCHANGE OF LICENSES AND ADDITIONAL LICENSES AND AFFILIATIONS

Licensed real estate brokers, upon submission of proper applications and payment of additional license and Guaranty Fund fees, may also obtain real estate salesperson or associate broker licenses and become affiliated with other licensed real estate brokers. They must, however, first obtain a commitment for such affiliation from each such broker and each must be informed of other licenses and affiliations. Brokers may also operate more than one real estate company, but they must obtain a separate real estate broker's license and pay an additional Guaranty Fund fee for each additional real estate brokerage company.

Licensees who hold salesperson, associate broker or broker licenses may exchange those licenses for other levels of license by complying with procedures established by the Commission and paying the required fees. Affiliates may obtain additional licenses and become affiliated with additional Maryland brokers by obtaining a commitment from each additional broker, paying the required additional licensing fees and Guaranty Fund assessments and giving notice of such multiple relationships to all their brokers. When all requirements have been met, the Commission will grant the appropriate additional licenses and issue additional license certificates and pocket cards.

Figure 1. Fees

The proper amount of fees must accompany every application. These fees are established by statute and as such are subject to change by the General Assembly. Total fees payable to the Commission are

	Original License Fee	Guaranty Fund Assessment*	Total Original Fees	Renewal or Exchange of License Fee
Broker	$95	$20	$115	$95
Assoc. Broker	$65	$20	$85	$65
Salesperson	$45	$20	$65	$45

Applicants are also required to pay the testing service a $46 examination fee to register to take or retake any real estate examination. Standard examination registration fees, which are neither refundable nor transferrable, may be paid by check, money order, company check or cashier's check. Cash is not accepted.

Fees for other services:

Taking a broker examination	$10
Taking a salesperson examination	10
Change of office or place of business	5
Change of name on licensee's records	5
Transfer of salesperson license to new broker	10
Issue duplicate license (when original is lost or destroyed)	5
Issue duplicate pocket card (when original is lost or destroyed)	1
Return checks for lack of funds	25
Certify licensure	10
Issue Branch Office Certificate	5
Reissue license (when it has been on inactive status)	10
Reinstate license (when it has not been timely renewed)	100

* This assessment is paid upon issuance (but not renewal) of any license.

TERM, RENEWAL AND TRANSFER OF LICENSES

Not later than one month before their licenses expire, the Commission mails to licensees renewal application forms and notices that state the dates on which the current licenses expire, the dates by which the Commission must receive the renewal applications—when licensees use hardcopy (paper) applications for renewal—and the amount of the renewal fees. The Commission will continue to process hardcopy applications. The preferred mode of application and renewal will be on-line via the Internet—a method designed to produce instantaneous processing. When licensees are real estate brokers, the Commission mails the renewal application form and notice to their principal offices. Notices of the need to renew are mailed to the residences of affiliates. It is essential that licensees keep the Commission updated on any changes in their home addresses.

Timely renewal is made before licenses expire. Those renewing must pay to the Commission the required renewal fees and complete the required number of hours of continuing education. Those renewing after the expiration date or completing the required number of hours of continuing education after the expiration date must pay a $100 reinstatement fee. They may apply for reinstatement at any time within four years after the expiration date.

They must then give proof of meeting all applicable continuing education require-ments for the period since expiration and pay past-due renewal fees as well as the reinstatement fee. They must also meet the requirement of good character and reputa-tion. Neither timely nor late renewal of a license affects the power of the Commis-sion to bring charges for prior acts or conduct.

DISHONORED CHECKS

A $25 collection fee is charged by the Commission for each dishonored check rendered. The original fee is not consid-ered paid until both the original fee and the collection fee are paid.

CONTINUING EDUCATION

Generally, all licensees must complete 15 clock hours of continuing education before renewing their licenses. While staggered renewal is being phased in—from 1998 to 2000—the number of hours required will be prorated according to the length of the license just ending. For example: a li-censee who received a 6-month renewal in early 1998 will need three hours and one who received a 30-month renewal will need 18 hours for renewal at the end of those respective terms. The Commission will announce the requirements for each interval in between those extremes. In all cases, at lease three hours of education in Category A—"Legislative Update"—is required. Continuing education is computed on the basis of clock hours with credit allowed only for individual courses of not less than 1½—and not more than six—hours in length.

Beginning with the renewal of their full two-year licenses granted in the year 2000, individuals who were licensed on October 1, 1998, and have held real estate licenses for ten years or more, need complete only six hours of continuing education for each renewal. The entire six hours must be in Category A.

To be approved by the Commission, all continuing education course subject matter must relate to real estate. Every renewal requires at least one three-hour course that outlines relevant changes that have occurred in federal, state or local legisla-tion and regulation during the preceding five years—Category A. There are several categories of subject matter approved for these courses:

A - Federal, State or local legislative issues

B - Antitrust law

C - Fair Housing law

D - Real estate ethics or professional standards

E - Disclosure

F - Professional enhancement for practicing licensees

G - Technology relating to real estate brokerage services (Not more than 3 hours per renewal)

Approved courses may be presented by the Maryland Association of REALTORS® or its member boards, the Real Estate Brokers of Baltimore City, Inc. or any similar professional association or an educational institution approved by the State Board of Higher Education. Continuing education courses must be taught by qualified instructors who are experienced in the real estate industry. The Commission's guidelines require instructors to have a minimum of three years' experience in specialized areas of expertise.

Upon completion of a continuing education course by a licensee, the training institution that conducted the course issues students certificates of completion stating the number of clock hours, name of the course taken and code letter of the subject category. The education provider also reports these facts electronically to the Commission. Licensees may then view their individual records of accumulated continuing education by accessing their personal file through the Commission's web site. To ensure the privacy of these data, licensees have their own Personal Identification Numbers—"PINs." These electronic records of training make it unnecessary for licensees to mail their certificates of completion of education to

the Commission at the time they apply for renewal.

The Commission may waive continuing education requirements for licensees who show good cause for being unable to meet the requirement.

INACTIVE STATUS

Upon the request of licensees the Commission places their licenses on inactive status if they surrender their certificates and pocket cards to the Commission. The Commission will place the licenses of associate real estate brokers and real estate salespersons on inactive status when they are no longer affiliated with licensed real estate brokers, upon the return of their certificates and cards to the Commission. A licensee whose license is on inactive status may not provide real estate brokerage services through that license. The placement of a license on inactive status does not affect the power of the Commission to suspend or revoke the license or to take any other disciplinary action against the licensee. Unless a license is reactivated, the license expires four years after the date it is placed on inactive status.

A licensee whose license is on inactive status remains responsible for renewing that license as required. Subject to the four-year limitation, a licensee may renew a license while it is on inactive status without complying with the continuing education requirements. Such renewal does not constitute reactivation. The Commission will reactivate the license of real estate brokers on inactive status and reissue license certificates and pocket cards to such brokers if they request reactivation and pay to the Commission the $10 reissuance fee. They must also meet the continuing education requirements that would have been necessary for renewal of licenses had they not been on inactive status. Salespersons and associate brokers returning from inactive status must meet the same requirements and also submit an affiliation commitment, contingent on their reactivation, from a broker.

DISPLAY OF LICENSE CERTIFICATES; LOSS OR DESTRUCTION

Licensed real estate brokers are required to display their license certificates at all times and in a conspicuous place in their offices. The license certificates of licensees who are affiliated with a real estate broker must be displayed at the office location out of which each usually works. The Commission must immediately be notified of the loss or destruction of a license certificate or pocket card. Upon receipt of an affidavit of loss or destruction and payment of the required fee, the Commission will issue appropriate duplicates.

CHANGE OF NAME

When a licensee or a firm takes a new name, on receipt of the required $5 application fee, the old certificate, pocket card and any required documentation, the Commission issues to the licensee a new license certificate and pocket card that reflect such change.

DEATH OF REAL ESTATE BROKER

On the death of a licensed real estate broker, any adult member of the family may carry on the brokerage for up to six months to close and terminate the business. In order for this to be done the certificate and pocket card of the deceased broker must be surrendered to the Commission and any information required by the Commission submitted.

Before the end of the six-month period for carrying on the business of a deceased real estate broker, an individual doing so may qualify for and receive from the Commission the license of the deceased broker, if the individual is a member of the immediate family of the decedent, has been continuously licensed as a real estate salesperson for the immediately preceding three years, passes the real estate broker examination required by this subtitle, and surrenders his or her real estate salesperson license certificate and pocket card to the Commission. There must also have been compliance with the qualifications for carrying on the business as stated in the previous paragraph.

A person receiving the reissued license of a deceased real estate broker may hold and use that license as long as four years without meeting the 135-hour educational requirement. However, if the requirement has not been met by that time, the license automatically expires.

RETURN OF LICENSES TO COMMISSION AND TERMINATION OF AFFILIATION

Upon the request or death of a real estate salesperson or associate real estate broker or after a hearing before the Commission, and upon a finding by the Commission that the license of a real estate salesperson or associate broker should be suspended or revoked, real estate brokers are required to surrender to the Commission, promptly on demand, any such person's license that may be in their possession or control. Failure to do so is grounds for disciplinary action.

If the affiliation between a real estate broker and a real estate salesperson or an associate real estate broker terminates, the real estate broker immediately must mail to the licensee at the last known address of that individual notice of such termination; submit written notice to the Commission, including a copy of the notice mailed to the licensee; and return the license certificate of the licensee to the Commission.

LICENSING OF OUT-OF-STATE APPLICANTS

The Commission will issue licenses only to nonresident applicants who file with the Commission a written consent that service of process on the executive director of the Commission shall bind the applicant in any action, suit or proceeding brought against the applicant, in any county in which the cause of action arose or the plaintiff resides. This **irrevocable consent** must be signed by the applicant. When serving process on the executive director of the Commission, the person filing must immediately send a copy of the filing, by certified mail, to the principal office of the person against whom the action is directed.

NOTE: The signature block on license examination applications contains these words: "If the address of this registration is not within the State of Maryland, I do hereby irrevocably consent that suits and actions may be commenced against me in the proper courts of the State of Maryland as required by the Maryland Annotated Code." Should any nonresident real estate broker or other such licensee participate in any real estate transaction or divide fee(s) and/or hold deposits from any such transaction in this state, this act, in itself, is considered to give the same irrevocable consent.

HANDLING OF COMPLAINTS ABOUT LICENSEES

Upon the Commission's receipt of a properly completed complaint form, it sends a copy of the complaint to the broker of record by the Commission's executive director, along with a letter stating that the broker must render, in writing, a full explanation as to the allegations and what action the broker recommends. The broker's failure to reply within 20 days of receipt of the letter may be considered a violation that could result, after a hearing, in the suspension or revocation of the broker's license or the assessment of a fine. A copy of the letter is also sent to the complainant. Upon receipt of the broker's response, a reply is sent to the complainant along with a copy of the broker's reply.

The Commission commences proceedings when a complaint is made by a Commission member or by other persons who must make them under oath. Complaints must be in writing, state specifically the facts on which the complaint is based, and may be accompanied by documentary or other evidence. After review a complaint may be referred for investigation if it appears an infraction has occurred. A complaint not referred for investigation is considered dismissed. Within 30 days of such dismissal any member of the Commission may file an exception to such dismissal. The full Commission then holds a hearing as to whether to proceed with an investigation. If an exception is not filed, the dismissal is considered a final decision of the Commission, and any party aggrieved by the decision to dismiss may appeal to the appropriate court. If the Commission or its designee determines that grounds exist for disciplinary action, the matter is referred for a hearing. A complaint not referred for a hearing after investigation must be dismissed. Any party aggrieved by that dismissal may also make a judicial appeal.

HEARINGS AND NOTICES

Except as otherwise provided in the State Government Article, before the Commission takes any final action it gives the individual against whom the action is contemplated an opportunity for a hearing before the Commission or a hearing board. At least ten days before the hearing, the hearing notice is served personally on the individuals or sent by certified mail to their last known addresses. If the individuals are licensees other than a broker, at least ten days before the hearing the Commission shall serve notice of the hearing to each real estate broker with whom the licensees are affiliated. The individuals may have attorneys represent them at hearings. If the individuals against whom the action is contemplated fail or refuse to appear, the Commission may proceed to hear and determine the matter without their presence. These hearings are open to the public.

Real Estate Hearing Board

The Commission establishes real estate hearing boards consisting of at least three members; at least one shall be a professional member and at least one, a consumer member. From among the hearing board members, the Commission designates a chairman.

Referral of Cases; Procedures Before Hearing Board

The Commission may order a hearing for any complaint that has been filed with the Commission and any other matter for which a hearing may be required.

A hearing board may exercise the same powers and shall conduct hearings for the Commission. The board determines if there is a reasonable basis to believe that there are grounds for disciplinary action against an applicant or licensee. If it finds a reasonable basis, it holds a hearing on the matter and files its conclusions with the Commission. The board advises the Commission specifically of any action brought against a licensee as a result of monetary loss, misappropriation of funds or fraud. If it does not find a reasonable basis, the hearing board dismisses the complaint.

Hearing Regulations

Regulations provide for four types of hearings: Judicial Hearings, Applications for Licensure, Revocation or Suspension of Licenses, and Claims Against the Guaranty Fund. Hearings are conducted under several levels of overlapping hearing regulations.

The decision of a hearing board is *final*. This means that any aggrieved party may then make a judicial appeal.

Upon dismissal of a complaint, the complainant and the licensee are notified in writing. The dismissal of a complaint after investigation is not reviewable further. Other complaints substantially based on the same facts are similarly dismissed unless additional facts come to light that would contradict the reasons for the earlier dismissal.

SUMMARY REVOCATION OF LICENSES BASED ON ACTIONS OF OTHER AGENCIES

The Commission may summarily (before holding a hearing) order the revocation of the license of any licensee if the licensee is convicted of a violation of this title, the conviction is final and the period for appeal has expired. The license of any non-resident licensee may be revoked if the real estate regulatory agency of the state where the licensee is a resident revokes the license issued by that state and certifies the order of revocation to the Commission.

When the Commission orders a summary revocation under this section, it gives licensees written notice of the revocation and the finding on which it was based. After the revocation is effective, the Commission grants them an opportunity to be heard promptly either before the Commission or before a hearing board. Rather than summarily order revocation of a license under this section, the Commission may elect not to revoke the license until after the licensee is given an opportunity for a hearing. If the Commission elects to give the licensee an opportunity for a hearing before revoking the license, the Commission gives notice and holds the hearing in the same manner as required for other hearings.

In any hearing held because of conviction or revocation by other agencies, the Commission considers only evidence of whether the alleged conviction or revocation in fact occurred. In any hearing held on these grounds, a licensee may present matters in mitigation of the offense charged.

SUMMARY SUSPENSION OF LICENSES FOR TRUST FUND VIOLATIONS

The Commission may—but is not required to—summarily order the suspension of a license if the licensee fails to account promptly for any funds held in trust or, on demand, fails to display to the Commission all records, books and accounts of any funds held in trust. The Commission gives the licensee notice and reasons as described above, and the opportunity to be heard later.

A summary suspension ordered by the Commission may start immediately or at any later date, as set by the order, and shall continue until the licensee complies with the conditions set forth by the Commission in its order or until the Commission orders a different disposition after a hearing held under this section.

JUDICIAL REVIEW

Any party who strongly disagrees with a final decision of the Commission may make an appeal to the circuit court. Upon the filing of a bond by the licensee, a circuit court may grant a stay (delay) of suspension or revocation of license. The court may set the bond required in any amount up to $50,000. The bond money would be for the use and benefit of any member of the public who might suffer financial loss because of any violation of the Brokers Act by the licensee.

NOTICE OF REVOCATION OR SUSPENSION

Whenever the Commission revokes or suspends a license and a stay is not ordered by the Commission or a court, the Commission notifies the licensee, the real estate broker with whom the licensee is affiliated, the Maryland Association of REALTORS®, the local Board or Association of REALTORS®, and the Realtist organization in the area of the licensee's office.

If the Commission revokes or suspends the license of a nonresident licensee, the Commission also notifies the Real Estate Commission or other licensing authority in the state where the licensee is a resident, reporting the cause for the revocation or suspension of the license.

REAL ESTATE GUARANTY FUND

The Commission has established a real estate Guaranty Fund and is required to maintain it at a level of at least $250,000.

Use of Monies Collected

The Commission deposits all money collected for the Guaranty Fund with the State treasurer, who invests it in the way the money in the State employees' retirement and pension systems is invested. The investment earnings are credited to the Guaranty Fund.

Initial Assessment for Fund

Before issuing licenses to applicants, the Commission requires them to pay $20 assessments, which are credited to the Guaranty Fund. Regardless of how many times an individual applies to the Commission for one level of license, the Commission makes only one such assessment. An exception is the situation in which a licensee is granted overlapping multiple licenses of the same or different levels, and so has to pay multiple assessments.

If the amount in the Guaranty Fund falls below $250,000, the Commission assesses all the individuals then holding licenses a fee sufficient to return the Guaranty Fund to that level.

Claims Against the Fund

A person may recover compensation from the Guaranty Fund only for actual financial losses. The claim must be based on an act or omission that occurs in the provision of real estate brokerage services by a licensee or an unlicensed employee of a licensed real estate broker. A claim must involve a transaction that relates to real estate located in the State and be based on an act or omission in which money or property is obtained from a person by theft, embezzlement, false pretenses, forgery or an act that constitutes fraud or misrepresentation. The amount recovered for any one claim against the Guaranty Fund may not exceed $25,000. A claim against the Guaranty Fund must be in writing, be made under oath, state the amount of loss claimed, state the facts on which the claim is based and be accompanied by documentation or other evidence that supports the claim. At any claim hearing the burden of proof shall be on the claimant to establish the validity of the claim.

A person may not recover from the Guaranty Fund any loss that relates to the purchase of any interest in a limited partnership that invests in real estate, a joint venture that is promoted by a real estate licensee for the purpose of investment in real estate or the purchase of commercial paper secured by real estate. A claim under the Guaranty Fund may not be filed by the spouse or by the personal representative of the licensee or the unlicensed employee alleged to be responsible for the act or omission giving rise to the claim. Any claim must be filed with the Commission within three years of the loss or damage.

Notice to Buyer

Real estate brokers must include in each sales contract they use in providing brokerage services a written notice that buyers are protected by the Guaranty Fund in an amount not more than $25,000.

Action by Commission on a Claim

The Commission acts promptly upon receiving claims by forwarding copies to licensees and/or unlicensed employees alleged to be responsible and to their brokers. The Commission then requires a written response, within 10 days, from each of those individuals concerning the allegations set forth in the claim. The Commission reviews the claim and any responses to the claim and is authorized to conduct an investigation. On the basis of this review and any investigation it conducts, the Commission schedules a hearing or dismisses the claim. If the claim is $3,000 or less, the Commission may issue a proposed order either to pay or to deny the claim. Both the claimant and the licensee receive a copy of this proposed order. Within 30 days either of them may request a hearing or file written exceptions to the order. If either happens, the Commission must schedule a hearing on the claim. If no hearing is requested and no exceptions taken, the proposed order becomes a final order of the Commission.

The Commission gives the claimant and the licensee or the unlicensed employee alleged

to be responsible notice of the hearing and an opportunity to participate in it before the Commission. The Commission must send the required notices to every party involved before conducting the hearing.

When the person alleged to be responsible is a licensee, the Commission combines this hearing with disciplinary proceedings against the licensee arising from the same facts alleged in the claim. The claimant can be a *party* to that part of the proceedings about the claim but may be only a *witness* in the disciplinary portion. The penalty for knowingly making a false statement or a material misstatement of fact about a Guaranty Fund matter is a fine of not more than $5,000 or imprisonment not exceeding one year or both.

Payments by the Guaranty Fund

If a claim proves valid, the Commission orders its payment by the Guaranty Fund. The amount of compensation recoverable from the Guaranty Fund is limited to the actual monetary loss incurred by the claimant. The payout may never be more than $25,000 for any one claim. The amount paid may not include losses other than those from the originating transaction; it may not reimburse for commissions owed to a licensee acting as either a principal or an agent in a real estate transaction; and it may not cover any attorney's fees incurred in seeking money from the Fund.

Payment is not made until either the time for seeking judicial review is over or any judicial stay has expired. The Commission orders payment of claims in the order in which they were awarded.

Reimbursement of the Guaranty Fund

After payment of a claim by the Guaranty Fund, the licensee responsible is required to reimburse the Fund in full for the amount paid and for interest of at least 10 percent. Each licensee responsible for the claim is jointly and severally liable. If licensees do not reimburse the Guaranty Fund as provided, the Commission may sue them for the amount that has not been reimbursed and seek liens against their real property.

When payment is made from the Fund, the Commission immediately and without further proceedings suspends the licenses of the offending licensees. Licensees suspended in this way are not reinstated until the licensees repay the full amounts owed to the Fund, plus interest, and make formal application for reinstatement. Reimbursement of the Fund does not affect any disciplinary actions imposed on or sanctions taken against licensees.

PROHIBITED ACTS AND PENALTIES

After holding the required hearing, the Commission is empowered to deny a license to any applicants and to reprimand, suspend or revoke the licenses of any licensees if they

1. fraudulently or deceptively obtain or attempt to obtain a license for themselves or others;

2. fraudulently or deceptively use licenses;

3. directly or through other persons willfully make misrepresentations or knowingly make false promises;

4. intentionally or negligently fail to disclose to any person with whom they deal a material fact that they know or should know that relates to property with which they deal;

5. as affiliates, provide or attempt to provide real estate brokerage services on behalf of real estate brokers without informing in writing any other real estate broker under whom the affiliate is licensed;

6. fail to follow the law concerning dual agency;

7. retain or attempt to retain the services of any unlicensed individuals as affiliates in an attempt to evade the law prohibiting payment of a commission to an unlicensed individual;

8. guarantee, authorize or permit other persons to guarantee future profits from the resale of real property;

9. solicit, sell or offer to sell real property so as to influence or attempt to influence a prospective party to the sale of real property by offering prizes or free lots, conducting a lottery or contest or advertising "free appraisals," unless prepared to appraise real estate free of charge for any person, for any purpose;

10. accept a listing contract to sell real property that fails to provide a definite termination date that is effective automatically without notice from the buyer or the seller;

11.	accept a listing contract to sell real property that provides for a "net" return to a seller and leaves the licensees free to sell the real property at any price higher than the "net" price;

12.	knowingly solicit a party to an exclusive listing contract with another licensee to terminate that contract and enter a new contract with the licensees making the solicitation;

13.	solicit a party to a sales contract, lease or agreement that was negotiated by other licensees to breach the contract, lease or agreement for the purpose of substituting a new contract, lease or agreement for which the licensees making the solicitation are either the real estate brokers or affiliated with those real estate brokers;

14.	for any transactions in which the licensees have served as or on behalf of a real estate broker, fail to furnish promptly to each party to the transaction copies of the listing contract to sell or rent real property, the contract of sale or the lease agreement;

15.	for any transactions in which the licensees have served as or on behalf of a real estate broker, fail to keep copies of all executed listing contracts to sell or rent real property, contracts of sale or lease agreements;

16.	whether or not acting for monetary gain, knowingly induce or attempt to induce persons to transfer real estate or discourage or attempt to discourage persons from buying real estate by making representations about the existing or potential proximity of real property owned or used by individuals of a particular race, color, religion, sex, handicap, familial status or national origin; or by representing that the existing or potential proximity of real property owned or used by individuals of a particular race, color, religion or national origin will or may result in: the lowering of property values, a change in the racial, religious or ethnic character of the block, neighborhood or area, an increase in criminal or antisocial behavior in the area or a decline in the quality of the schools serving the area;

17.	use any of the following material if it includes the name of an organization or association of which the licensees are not members: contract forms for the listing of real property for sale, rent or exchange; contract forms for the sale, rent or exchange of real property; or any advertising matter;

18.	as real estate brokers or affiliates, advertise the sale or rent of or an offer to buy real property while failing to disclose in the advertisement the name of the advertisers and the fact that the advertisers are real estate licensees;

19.	advertise in any misleading or untruthful manner;

20.	as affiliates, advertise the sale or rent of or an offer to buy real property in their names while failing to disclose in the advertisement the name of the real estate broker on whose behalf the affiliates are acting;

21. for real estate brokerage services provided by associate real estate brokers or real estate salespersons, accept commissions or other valuable considerations from persons other than real estate brokers with whom they are affiliated;

22. fail to account for or to remit promptly any money that comes into their possession;

23. pay or receive a rebate, profit, compensation or commission in violation of any provision of this Act;

24. under the laws of the United States or of any state, are convicted of felonies or misdemeanors that are directly related to their fitness and qualification to provide real estate brokerage services; or a crime that constitutes a violation of any provision of the Brokers Act;

25. engage in conduct that demonstrates bad faith, incompetency or untrustworthiness or that constitutes dishonest, fraudulent or improper dealings;

26. with actual knowledge of the violation, associate with licensees in a transaction or practice that violates any provision of the Brokers Act;

27. fail as real estate brokers to exercise reasonable and adequate supervision over the provision of real estate

brokerage services by other individuals on behalf of the broker;

28. provide to any parties contracts that do not contain a notice of a buyer's right of selection, as required by the Brokers Act;

29. require a buyer to employ a particular title insurance company, settlement company, escrow company or title lawyer in violation of this Act;

30. fail to make the disclosure of representation as required by §17-528;

31. violate any trust accounts provision of this Act that relates to trust money;

32. violate any other provision of this Act;

33. violate any regulation adopted under this Act or any provision of the Code of Ethics, or

34. violate §17-320(d) by failing as branch office managers to exercise reasonable and adequate supervision over the brokerage work of sales agents or associate brokers in their offices.

Instead of, or in addition to, suspension or revocation, the Commission may impose a penalty not exceeding $2,000 for each violation. To determine the amount of the penalty imposed, the Commission considers the seriousness of the violation, the harm caused by the violation, the good faith of the licensee, and any history of previous violations by the licensee. The Commission pays any penalty collected into the General Fund of the State.

The Commission considers the following facts in the granting, denial, renewal, suspension or revocation of licenses, or the reprimand of licensees, when they are convicted of felonies or misdemeanors: the nature of the crime, the relationship of the crime to the activities authorized by the license; with respect to a felony, the relevance of the conviction to the fitness and qualification of the applicants or licensees to provide real estate brokerage services; the length of time since the conviction; and the behavior and activities of the applicants or licensees before and after their convictions. The Drug Enforcement Act of 1990 authorizes the Commission to impose sanctions upon licensees for a controlled substance offense.

OTHER PROHIBITED ACTS

In addition to the prohibitions and penalties enumerated above, the Brokers Act provides for fines not to exceed $5,000 and/or imprisonment not to exceed one year for these additional acts. Note that the term *person* includes licensees, nonlicensees, individuals and business entities such as corporations, partnerships, limited liability companies, etc.

1. Except as otherwise provided in this Act, a person may not provide, attempt to provide, or offer to provide real estate brokerage services unless licensed by the Commission.

2. Unless authorized under this Act to provide real estate brokerage services, a person may not represent to the public by use of the title Licensed Real Estate Broker, Licensed Associ-

ate Real Estate Broker or Licensed Salesperson, by other title, by description of services, methods or procedures or otherwise that the person is authorized to provide real estate brokerage services in the State.

3. Real estate brokers may not allow other licensees or any other unauthorized individuals to provide real estate brokerage services independently as real estate brokers. Real estate brokers may not retain unlicensed individuals to provide real estate brokerage services on their behalf. Licensed real estate brokers may not lend their license certificates or pocket cards to other individuals.

4. Licensees may not pay any form of compensation for the provision of real estate brokerage services to persons not licensed under the Brokers Act, except that payment may be made to individuals who are licensed in another state and who meet the requirements of this Act. A professional service corporation formed under this Act may also receive such compensation.

5. Except as otherwise provided, licenses may not pay or offer to pay commissions to lawyers simply for the referral of persons as possible parties to residential real estate transactions. Licensees may not solicit referral business from lawyers by a mass solicitation that offers to pay fees or commissions to the lawyers. This does not apply to payments or offers of payments to lawyers who hold a real estate broker license under this Act or are otherwise entitled to a

commission. Other than the commissions expressly prohibited, the law does not prohibit the payment or the offer of a payment of a commission by a licensee to a lawyer for other services that relate to real estate transactions.

6. In a real estate transaction involving a single-family dwelling, licensees or lawyers acting as real estate brokers may not require buyers, as a condition of settlement, to employ a particular title insurance company, settlement company or escrow company, mortgage lender, financial institution, or title lawyer. However, a seller may make owner financing a condition of sale.

7. Whether or not acting for monetary gain, persons may not knowingly induce or attempt to induce other persons to sell or rent dwellings or otherwise transfer real estate or knowingly discourage or attempt to discourage other persons from purchasing real estate:

   • by making representations regarding the entry or prospective entry into a neighborhood of individuals of a particular race, color, sex, religion or national origin;

   • by making representations regarding the existing or potential proximity of real property owned or used by individuals of a particular race, color, sex, religion or national origin; or

   • by representing that the existing or potential proximity of real property owned or used by individuals of a particular race, color, sex, religion or national origin will or may result in: the lowering of property values; a change in the racial, religious or ethnic character of the block, neighborhood or area; an increase in criminal or antisocial behavior in the area; or a decline in the quality of schools serving the area.

8. Persons may not provide financial assistance by loan, gift or otherwise to other persons if they have actual knowledge that the financial assistance will be used in transactions that result from a fair housing violation.

9. If one of the purposes of the solicitation or attempted solicitation is to change the racial composition of a neighborhood, persons may not solicit or attempt to solicit the listing of residential properties for sale or lease by in-person door-to-door solicitation, telephone solicitation or mass distribution of circulars.

10. A corporation, partnership or any other association may not commit or cause any other person to commit any act that constitutes grounds for disciplinary action against a licensee under the Brokers Act. Violators are guilty of misdemeanors and, upon conviction, subject to a fine not exceeding $5,000.

11. In transactions involving residential property in Baltimore City:

    • All real estate brokers shall break down the properties listed in the registry into price categories established by the Commission. If a prospective buyer requests to see the registry, they shall allow the prospective buyer to see the part of the registry for the price category in which the prospective buyer indicates interest. This does not require a real estate broker who is a member of a multiple-listing service to disclose properties that are obtained from multiple listing.

• Unless requested to do so by a prospective buyer or renter, real estate licensees may not fail or refuse to show any residential property that is available for sale, rent or sublease to a prospective buyer or renter because of: the race, color, sex, religion, age or national origin of the prospective buyer or renter; the racial composition or character of the neighborhood where the property is located.

• Licensees may not fail or refuse to show all available listed residential properties that are in a certain area and within a specified price range to a prospective buyer or renter who has requested to be shown all available properties that are in the area and within the specified price range.

• If the representation is made because of the race, color, sex, religion, age, or national origin of the prospective buyer or renter, or because of the racial composition or character of the area where the property is located, real estate licensees may not represent to a prospective buyers or renters that the available residential properties, prospective sites for a resi-

dence or listings are limited to those already shown when, in fact, there is a residential property, a prospective site for a residence or a listing that is available and within the price range specified by the prospective buyer or renter. This does not prohibit a licensee from charging a reasonable fee for showing a residential property to a prospective buyer or renter.

The Commission enforces the provisions of this section concerning Baltimore City. For this purpose, it receives complaints, conducts investigations, issues subpoenas administers oaths and holds hearings.

12. In transactions involving residential property in Montgomery County:

• Real estate brokers shall maintain current and complete registries of all residential properties that they personally list for sale or rent in Montgomery County and, if members of a multiple-listing service, a registry of properties listed with the Montgomery County multiple-listing service.

• Licensees may not refuse to show any residential property or prospective site for a residence that is available for sale, rent or sublease to a prospective buyer or renter because of the race, color, religion, sex, marital status, national origin, physical or mental handicap of the prospective buyer or renter, or because of the composition or character of the neighborhood in which the property is located.

The Commission enforces the provisions of this section concerning Montgomery County. For this purpose it receives complaints, conducts investigations, issues subpoenas and holds hearings.

13. In Baltimore City and Baltimore County, real estate licensees may not mass-solicit listings by using the name or address of a present or previous client without the written consent of both parties to the contract involving that client.

Maryland courts are required to report to the Commission, for appropriate action, all convictions of licensees for violation of this Act with respect to blockbusting and discriminatory real estate practices in Baltimore City or Montgomery County.

REAL ESTATE BROKERAGE PRACTICE IN BALTIMORE CITY

Although Baltimore City does not issue or require a separate real estate license to perform real estate activities there, local law does regulate the activities of licensees who practice in that city. Many of the prohibited acts are similar, if not identical, to State law. The Baltimore City real estate license law is found in §132 of Article 19 of the Baltimore City Code under the title "Real Estate Practices."

MARYLAND SECURITIES ACT

The Maryland Securities Act requires licensing of persons engaged in the offer and sale of real estate–related securities, including limited partnership interests in real property. The Maryland Securities Commission regulates all activities construed to be securities-related business. To inquire if certain activities could be construed as securities-related business, contact the Maryland Securities Commissioner.

REAL ESTATE APPRAISERS ACT

Title 16 of the *Business Occupations and Professions Article* of the Annotated Code of Maryland establishes licensing and certification procedures for real estate appraisers and creates a nine-member State Commission of Real Estate Appraisers within the Department of Labor, Licensing and Regulation to administer that act.

Individuals who are licensed to provide real estate brokerage services do not also need to be licensed as real estate appraisers when merely recommending a listing price or a purchase price for real estate, provided that the opinion is not called an appraisal. A competitive market analysis (CMA) is not an appraisal, and its preparation for a seller or purchaser does not require an appraisal license or certificate.

To receive a real estate appraisers license or certification, an individual must complete mandated educational requirements, pass an examination developed by the State Commission of Real Estate Appraisers and have accumulated mandated hours of acceptable appraisal work experience.

An individual may hold a real estate license and at the same time be a licensed or certified real estate appraiser. Such individuals should be extremely careful to avoid any conflicts of interest that could arise from providing real estate appraisal services in transactions in which they, their friends, relatives or those employed by their broker are also agents or principals.

CHANGES IN THE LICENSE LAW AND REGULATIONS

Changes are occasionally made in the Brokers Act and the regulations of the Commission. The material included in this chapter is current as of the date of publication. However, readers are cautioned to ascertain whether changes have been made since publication of this volume. See the OVERVIEW section of this chapter for sources of updated information. Before the Commission adopts, amends or repeals regulations, it publishes notice of the proposed action in the *Maryland Register*, with an estimate of economic impact, a notice of opportunity for public comment on the proposal, and the text of the proposed changes. After 45 days, the Commission takes final action on the proposal. At that time a report of final action is published in the *Maryland Register*. The final action takes effect ten days after that notice appears, unless the Commission specifies a later date.

QUESTIONS

1. Licensed salespersons may represent

   a. any owners who directly employ them.
   b. not more than one owner at one time.
   c. only brokers under whom they are licensed.
   d. any broker who is duly licensed.

2. License certificates issued for salespersons must be

   a. carried by them at all times.
   b. displayed by their brokers in their brokerage offices.
   c. retained by the Real Estate Commission.
   d. displayed by them in their homes.

3. Brokers need NOT notify the Commission

   a. when salespersons resign.
   b. when there are changes in the locations of their offices.
   c. when there are changes in the names of their firms.
   d. of changes in commission sharing arrangements.

4. As a licensed salesperson you receive a lead from a friend who is not a real estate licensee. You would like to split your commission with your friend.

   a. This is a violation of the license law.
   b. This is NOT a violation of the license law.
   c. This is a violation of the license law only if the seller is NOT informed.
   d. This is a violation of the license law only if your broker has NOT given written permission.

5. A broker is appointed to sell a Maryland property through an exclusive-right-to-sell listing contract. The broker will be entitled to a commission

   a. only if she or one of her salespeople sells the property.
   b. if the property is sold during the listing period.
   c. only if the property is sold by the broker or the owner.
   d. only if the sale is made by a multiple-listing service.

6. Which of the following fees is paid bienni- ally?

    a. Guaranty Fund fee
    b. Broker's or salesperson's original license fee
    c. Broker's or salesperson's license renewal fee
    d. Guaranty Fund reassessment

7. In Maryland the act of "blockbusting" is

    a. unethical but NOT prohibited by law.
    b. a felony.
    c. a misdemeanor.
    d. a legitimate sales technique.

8. Individuals found guilty of operating in the real estate business without a license may be fined by

    a. the district attorney.
    b. a circuit court.
    c. the Board or Association of REALTORS®.
    d. the attorney general.

9. An unlicensed person improperly collecting a real estate commission is guilty of

    a. duress.
    b. a felony.
    c. a misdemeanor.
    d. fraud.

10. The Commission may revoke the license of any licensee who is found guilty of

    a. slandering competitors.
    b. intemperance.
    c. misrepresentation.
    d. violation of the motor vehicle code.

11. The maximum penalty for filing a false statement with the Commission in reference to the Guaranty Fund is

    a. NOT less than $200.
    b. NOT more than $200.
    c. $10,000 and up to two years' imprison- ment.
    d. $5,000 and up to one year's imprison- ment.

12. A license to provide real estate brokerage services can be issued only to a(n)

    a. corporation.
    b. limited liability company (LLC).
    c. partnership.
    d. individual.

13. Members of the Real Estate Commission of Maryland are appointed by the

    a. Maryland Senate.
    b. Governor
    c. House of Delegates.
    d. Executive Director of the Real Estate Commission.

14. A salesperson license issued by the Real Estate Commission on November 1 will expire

    a. one year from the date of issue.
    b. two years from the date of issue.
    c. April 30 of the next even-numbered year.
    d. March 1 of the next even-numbered year.

15. The main purpose of the Brokers Act is to

    a. raise revenue.
    b. protect the public interest.
    c. control salespersons.
    d. restrict competition.

16. The executive director of the Real Estate Commission is

    a. appointed by the Governor.
    b. confirmed by the State Senate.
    c. appointed by the Secretary.
    d. selected from the Maryland State Employees Classified System.

17. Real estate ads placed by licensees must include the

    a. name and address of the property owner.
    b. name of the listing salesperson.
    c. trade name of the broker.
    d. location of the property.

18. The Guaranty Fund must be maintained at a minimum of

    a. $250,000.   c. $2,000.
    b. $25,000.   d. $200,000.

19. The Code of Ethics is divided into three parts. Which of the following is NOT one of those parts?

    a. Relations to the public
    b. Relations to the Commission
    c. Relations to the client
    d. Relations to fellow licensees

20. The Real Estate Commission of Maryland is composed of

    a. five members.
    b. four persons who are NOT engaged in the real estate business as well as five licensees.
    c. four licensed and four unlicensed persons.
    d. members of the real estate boards or associations.

21. The Commission may refuse to issue a license to a Maryland resident who has filed a proper application and met the legal requirements

    a. after holding a hearing on the matter.
    b. if the applicant has been convicted of a traffic violation within the past year.
    c. without holding a hearing on the matter.
    d. if the applicant has not reached the age of 21 years.

22. License fees are established by the

    a. Real Estate Commission.
    b. Real Estate Board.
    c. Secretary of the Department of Labor, Licensing and Regulation.
    d. General Assembly.

23. Which of the following is an act of real estate brokerage that requires a real estate brokerage license?

    a. A mortgage loan institution sells real estate acquired through foreclosure.
    b. A person offers to sell real estate for a friend for a fee.
    c. An attorney-at-law, representing a spouse in a divorce action, helps sell a house the couple owns.
    d. A property owner subdivides his land and sells five lots in one calendar year.

24. Real estate license applicants pay the licensing fee to the

    a. Real Estate Commission of Maryland.
    b. testing service.
    c. Real Estate Board or Association.
    d. Comptroller of the State of Maryland.

25. Employees of the Commission

    a. include an executive director and field inspectors.
    b. must be licensed as brokers or salespeople while employed by the Commission.
    c. must have been licensed before being employed by the Commission.
    d. are permitted to perform acts of brokerage for which a license is required.

26. In Maryland, the person primarily responsible for the real estate brokerage services provided through a corporation is the

    a. president of the corporation.
    b. licensed real estate broker of the firm.
    c. chairman of the board.
    d. corporate attorney.

27. When brokers discharge salespersons, the licenses of the salespersons should be

    a. returned to the Real Estate Commission by the brokers.
    b. returned to the Real Estate Commission by the salespersons.
    c. removed from display but retained by the brokers.
    d. returned to the salespersons.

28. The Guaranty Fund protects a buyer for certain financial losses up to

    a. $250,000.   c. $2,500.
    b. $25,000.   d. Unlimited

Real Estate Agency and Brokerage

OVERVIEW

Agency in real estate brokerage bestows few powers upon licensee agents but imposes many responsibilities. Licensees performing real estate brokerage have always had common law fiduciary duties. Recent legislation assembles in one statute many aspects of common law affecting real estate brokerage. Issues not included in the statute are still governed by common law.

The Maryland Real Estate Brokers Act, Title 17 of the *Business Occupations and Professions Article* of the Annotated Code of Maryland (referred to throughout this volume as the *Brokers Act*), defines real estate brokerage as performing certain services for another person in return for consideration. These services are selling, buying, exchanging or leasing real estate; collecting rent for the use of any real estate; giving assistance in locating or obtaining for purchase any residential real estate; regularly dealing in real estate or in leases or options on real estate; promoting the sale of real estate through listing it in a publication issued primarily for promoting real estate sales; subdividing land and selling the divided lots; and acting as consultant in any of these activities.

AGENCY RELATIONSHIPS

Maryland real estate licensees owe their clients the fiduciary duties of care, obedience within the law, accounting, loyalty and disclosure. They owe customers, and other *third parties*, honest and fair dealing, appropriate care, prompt presentation of all offers and counteroffers, honest answers to all questions except those that are confidential to a client, and voluntary disclosure of material facts. Brokerage practices that reflect thorough understanding of the difference between client and customer duties tend to reduce regulatory complaints and much litigation.

~~Virtually all real estate brokerage companies in~~ Some real estate brokers Maryland offer to *assist* purchasers as *customers* in finding properties to purchase without representing them as *clients*. They also offer to *represent* owners as *clients* in the sale of properties. Understanding the difference between *client-level service* and *customer-level service* is fundamental to effective and lawful provision of real estate brokerage services. The student is strongly urged to learn the difference between the terms *represent* and *assist*. Licensees represent clients. They assist customers.

A great many firms in certain areas of the state now also offer to represent buyers by giving them client-level service. When a broker represents a buyer and presents property listed with another broker, the seller whose property is being presented is not a client of the selling broker. The seller is, however, receiving client-level service from the listing company. Both brokerage firms are providing single-agency service.

A more complex situation arises when the firm representing the buyer wants to present property *listed* with that company. To do so is *dual agency* because the firm is serving as agent of both the buyer and the seller in the same transaction. The desire of major firms to provide both buyer and seller representation has led to much discussion and legislation seeking to clarify how such dual agency may be accomplished and still offer effective service and protection to the public.

Maryland law requires that agreements to represent purchasers or lessees and to represent sellers or lessors in residential brokerage be in writing. An agency agreement to represent sellers or lessors (a "listing") must state the amount of the broker's compensation, either as a percentage or as a dollar amount, and fix a definite date on which the agreement will expire. This expiration must be effective without further notice from either party.

NOTE TO STUDENTS

To make reading easier, this text will generally use the term *buyers* rather than *buyers or lessees* and *sellers* rather than *sellers or lessors*. Statements about *property to purchase* generally also apply to *property to lease*. Students should understand that both meanings are intended in each case where they might reasonably apply.

BROKER OPTIONS IN REPRESENTATION

Licensed real estate brokers in Maryland may choose to operate either *single agency* or *dual agency* companies. Those operating as single agency companies typically choose to act as one of the following: a single agency company offering to represent either buyers or sellers, but not both, in any given transaction; an exclusive seller agency company, offering to represent only sellers in all transactions; or an exclusive buyer agency company, offering to represent only buyers in all transactions.

Single agency companies offer to represent sellers when prospective buyers for their property are customers (not clients) of that brokerage and when prospective buyers for the property are produced by cooperating competitor companies. The same single agency companies may also offer to represent buyers in dealing with properties listed with other companies. What they will not do is offer to represent buyers and sellers in the same property transaction.

Dual agency companies offer to represent sellers in dealing with buyers from other firms, but are willing to represent buyers who wish to consider properties *listed by their firm*. In such cases the firm is willing to perform *dual agency*. Maryland law allows brokers to engage in such dual agency on condition that they make timely and meaningful written disclosure of their dual status to all parties to every such transaction, secure the informed consent of all parties and appoint one *intra-company* agent—a salesperson or associate broker in the firm—to represent the buyers and a different intra-company agent to represent the sellers in the same transaction.

It is essential for each company to decide which agency service or services it will offer and present its policy and associated procedures to everyone in the organization. All persons affiliated with the company should be trained in the proper perform- ance of these services. It is the responsi- bility of licensees who manage offices to ensure that these services are being performed according to the detailed requirements of the Brokers Act.

TYPES OF REPRESENTATION

The Brokers Act recognizes and defines several kinds of agency representation in real estate brokerage: buyer's agent, cooperating agent, intra-company agent, dual agent, and seller's agent.

- *Buyer's agents* are licensees who *represent* prospective *buyers* in the acquisition of real estate. This arrangement is a national trend and is becoming increasingly common in many parts of Maryland. When representing buyers in acquiring a property listed with another com- pany, *buyer's agents are not subagents of the owner-seller*. Nor are they cooperating agents as described in the paragraph below.

- *Cooperating agents* are licensees who are not affiliated with or acting as a listing real estate broker for a property. Rather, they work as subagents, *representing the owner* through and under that owner's listing broker. They *assist* pro- spective *buyers* in the acquisition of real estate. This has long been a typical arrangement in transactions that involve a listing brokerage firm and a selling brokerage firm. It remains a common practice.

- *Intra-company agents* are licensees affiliated with a broker and desig- nated by that broker to act ~~as dual agents~~ on behalf of either a seller or a buyer in the purchase or sale of real estate listed with their com- pany.

- *Dual agents* are brokers, or their office managers designees who *represent* not only sellers but also prospective purchasers in one property transaction. If all parties sign the *Consent for Dual Agency* form, presented in Figure 4/5.2, they agree that they understand and are willing to accept dual agency.

- *Seller's agents* are licensees who are affiliated with or acting as the listing broker for real estate. They *represent* the seller and *assist* prospective buyers in the acquisi- tion of that real estate.

Figure 4/5.1 Commission's Agency Relationship Information Form (Page 1 of 2)

January 1, 1999

STATE OF MARYLAND
REAL ESTATE COMMISSION

Understanding Whom Real Estate Agents Represent

Before you decide to sell or buy or rent a home you need to consider the following information:

Agents Who Represent the Seller

Seller's Agent: A seller's agent works for the real estate company that lists and markets the property for the sellers, or landlords, and exclusively represents the sellers or landlords. That means that he or she may assist the buyer or tenant in purchasing or renting the property, but his or her duty of loyalty is only to the sellers or landlords. The seller pays the seller's agent's fee as specified in a written listing agreement.

Cooperating Agent: A cooperating agent works for a real estate company different from the company for which the seller's agent works. The cooperating agent can assist a buyer or tenant in purchasing or renting a property, but his or her duty of loyalty is only to the sellers or landlords. The cooperating agent's fee is paid by the sellers or landlords through the seller's agent's company.

Agents Who Represent the Buyer

Presumed Buyer's Agent (no written agreement): When a person goes to a real estate agent for assistance in finding a home to buy or rent, the agent is presumed to be representing the buyer and can show the buyer properties that are *not* listed by the agent's real estate company. A presumed buyer's agent may *not* make or prepare an offer or negotiate a sale for the buyer. The buyer does *not* have an obligation to pay anything to the presumed agent.

If for any reason the buyer does not want the agent to represent him or her as a presumed agent, either *initially* or *at any time*, the buyer can decline or terminate a presumed agency relationship simply by saying so.

Buyer's Agent (by written agreement): A buyer or tenant may enter into a written contract with a real estate agent which provides that the agent will represent the buyer or tenant in locating a property to buy or rent. The agent is then known as the buyer's agent. That agent assists the buyer in evaluating properties and preparing offers, and negotiates in the best interests of the buyer or tenant. The agent's fee is paid according to the written agreement between the agent and the buyer or tenant. If you as a buyer or tenant wish to have an agent represent you exclusively, you must enter into a written buyer agency agreement

Dual Agents

The possibility of **dual agency** arises when the buyer's agent and the seller's agent both work for the same real estate company, and the buyer is interested in property listed by that company. The real estate company, or broker, is called the "dual agent." Dual agents do not act exclusively in the interests of either the seller or buyer, or landlord or tenant, and therefore cannot give undivided loyalty to either party. There may be a conflict of interest because the interests of the seller and buyer may be different or adverse.

If both seller and buyer, or landlord and tenant, agree to dual agency by signing a Consent For Dual Agency form, then the real estate company (the "dual agent") will assign one agent to represent the seller or landlord (the seller's "intra-company agent") and another agent to represent the buyer or tenant (the buyer's "intra-company agent"). Intra-company agents may provide the same services to their clients as exclusive seller's or buyer's agents, including advising their clients as to price and negotiation strategy, provided the clients have both consented to be represented by dual agency.

Figure 4/5.1 Commission's Agency Relationship Information Form (Page 2 of 2)

If either party does not agree to dual agency, the real estate company may withdraw the agency agreement for that particular property with either the buyer or seller, or both. If the seller's agreement is terminated, the seller must then either represent him or herself or arrange to be represented by an agent from another real estate company.   If the buyer's agreement is terminated, the buyer or tenant may choose to enter into a written buyer agency agreement with an agent from a different company. Alternatively, the buyer or tenant may choose not to be represented by an agent of his or her own but simply to receive assistance from the seller's agent, from another agent in that company, or from a cooperating agent from another company.

No matter what type of agent you choose to work with, you have the following rights and responsibilities in selling or buying or renting property:

➢ Real estate agents are obligated by law to treat all parties to a real estate transaction honestly and fairly. They must exercise reasonable care and diligence and maintain the confidentiality of clients. They must not discriminate in the offering of properties; they must promptly present each written offer or counteroffer to the other party; and they must answer questions truthfully.

➢ Real estate agents must disclose all material facts that they know or should know relating to a property. An agent's duty to maintain confidentiality does not apply to the disclosure of material facts about a property.

➢ All agreements with real estate agents should be in writing and should explain the duties and obligations of the agent. The agreement should explain how the agent will be paid and any fee-sharing agreements with other agents.

➢ You have the responsibility to protect your own interests. You should carefully read all agreements to make sure they accurately reflect your understanding. A real estate agent is qualified to advise you on real estate matters only. If you need legal or tax advice, it is your responsibility to consult a licensed attorney or accountant.

Any complaints about a real estate agent may be filed with the Real Estate Commission at 500 North Calvert Street, Baltimore, MD 21202. (410) 230-6200.

This notice is information required by law and is NOT A CONTRACT

We, the ❑ Sellers/Landlord ❑ Buyers/Tenants acknowledge receipt of a copy of this disclosure and

that _____ (firm name)

and _____ (salesperson) are working as:

❑ seller/landlord's agent
❑ cooperating agent
❑ buyer's agent
❑ dual agent (See Consent for Dual Agency form)
(You may check more than one box)

_____   _____
Signature   Date   Signature   Date

I certify that on this date I made the required agency disclosure to the individuals identified below and they were unable or unwilling to acknowledge receipt of a copy of this disclosure statement.

_____
Signature of agent   Date

_____   _____
Name of individual to whom disclosure was made   Name of individual to whom disclosure was made

Figure 4/5.2 Commission's Consent for Dual Agency (Page 1 of 2)

January 1, 1999

STATE OF MARYLAND
REAL ESTATE COMMISSION

Consent For Dual Agency

(In this form, the word "seller" includes "landlord", "buyer" includes "tenant", and "purchase" or "sale" includes "lease.")

When Dual Agency May Occur

The possibility of dual agency arises when:

> ➤ The buyer is interested in a property listed by a real estate company; and

> ➤ The seller's agent and the buyer's agent work for that same real estate company.

Before the buyer and seller can proceed to be represented by a dual agent, they must both sign a Consent For Dual Agency. If they have previously signed a Consent For Dual Agency, they must affirm their consent for the sale of a particular property to a particular buyer.

Important Considerations Before Making a Decision About Dual Agency

☞ A dual agent does not exclusively represent either the seller or buyer and there may be a conflict of interest because the interests of the seller and buyer may be different or adverse.

☞ As a dual agent, the real estate company does not owe undivided loyalty to either the seller or buyer.

Your Choices Concerning Dual Agency

When a dual agency situation in fact arises, the buyer and seller have the following options:

1. Consent in writing to dual agency. If all parties consent in writing, the real estate company (the "dual agent") will assign one real estate agent from the company to represent the seller or landlord (the seller's "intra-company agent") and another agent from the company to represent the buyer or tenant (the buyer's "intra-company agent"). Intra-company agents may provide the same services to their clients as an exclusive seller's or buyer's agent, including advising their clients as to price and negotiation strategy.

2. Do not consent to dual agency. If either the buyer or the seller, or landlord or tenant, refuses to consent in writing to dual agency, the real estate company must terminate the agency agreement for that particular property with either the buyer or the seller, or both. If the seller's agreement is terminated, the seller must then either represent him or herself or arrange to be represented by an agent from another real estate company. If the buyer's agreement is terminated, the buyer or tenant may choose to enter into a written buyer agency agreement with an agent from a different company. Alternatively, the buyer or tenant may choose not to be represented by an agent of his or her own but simply to receive assistance from the seller's agent, from another agent in that company, or from a cooperating agent from another company.

Figure 4/5.2 Commission's Consent for Dual Agency (Page 2 of 2)

Duties of a Dual Agent and Intra-Company Agent

Like other agents, dual agents and intra-company agents must keep confidential information about a client's bargaining position or motivations unless the client gives consent to disclose the information. For example, a dual agent or intra-company agent may not tell the other party, or the other party's agent, without consent of the client:

- ➤ anything the client asks to be kept confidential*,
- ➤ that the seller would accept a lower price or other terms,
- ➤ that the buyer would accept a higher price or other terms,
- ➤ the reasons why a party wants to sell or buy, or
- ➤ that a party needs to sell or buy quickly.

*However, like all agents, a dual agent and intra-company agent must disclose any material facts about a property to the other party.

How Dual Agents Are Paid

Only the dual agent receives compensation on the sale of a property listed by that company.

If a financial bonus is offered to an agent who sells property that is listed with his company, this fact must be disclosed in writing to both the buyer and seller.

I have read the above information, and I understand the terms of the dual agency. I understand that I do not have to consent to a dual agency, and that if I do not consent, there will not be a dual agency. I hereby voluntarily consent to have

_____ act as dual agent for me as the:
(Firm Name)

❑ seller in the sale of the property at: _____.

❑ buyer in the purchase of any property listed for sale with the above-referenced firm.

| _____ | _____ | _____ | _____ |
| Signature | Date | Signature | Date |

AFFIRMATION

The undersigned Seller(s) hereby affirms consent to Dual Agency:

| _____ | _____ | _____ | _____ |
| Signature | Date | Signature | Date |

The undersigned Buyer(s) hereby affirms consent to dual agency:

| _____ | _____ | _____ |
| Signature | Date | Property location |

| _____ | _____ |
| Signature | Date |

PRESUMED BUYER REPRESENTATION

The Maryland Brokers Act states that effective January 1, 1999, members of the public who approach a licensee for help in finding a property to buy are *presumed to be clients of the company of that licensee*. This is what many home buyers had often thought to be the case anyway, according to research conducted by the Federal Trade Commission.

A licensee's *presumed agency representation* of the buyers ends when

- either the licensee or the buyers reject the presumed relationship;
- the buyers want to make an offer to purchase a property; or
- the buyers wish to consider a property listed with the licensee's company.

In either of the last two instances, the licensee must then present buyers with the form—*Understanding Whom Real Estate Agents Represent*—issued by the Commission. See Figure 4/5.1. On this form, the buyers can indicate their choice either to be treated as customers or as clients.

If the buyers choose to become clients, a further choice is required as to whether they will agree to dual agency, which would arise if they were shown property listed with their agent's firm. This latter choice also is recorded on another form mandated by the Commission—*Consent for Dual Agency*. See Figure 4/5.2. Buyers who reject representation but wish to continue to be assisted, will receive customer-level treatment. Any facts learned from them during the period of presumed buyer representation must be kept confidential by the licensee and not used to their disadvantage in any later negotiations.

A firm may make it a policy for affiliates to present the choice between customer and client status very early in their contacts with prospects. This disclosure does not end the presumed buyer representation if no choice is made by the prospect. However, once made, the decision—either to enter into a buyer representation agreement with the company or to reject representation—would end any presumed buyer representation with its attendant fiduciary duties.

A firm that chooses to avoid presumed buyer representation may require its affiliates to make immediate disclosure of the agency alternatives available to prospects and refuse to continue in the presumed buyer representation role.

If a firm allows its affiliates to continue to act as presumed buyer representatives after presenting the information forms, the law does not require that prospects sign the form at that time. However, before the licensee working with them can present any written offer on their behalf or even show them a property listed within that firm, prospects must make a written choice about representation.

Affiliates acting under presumed buyer representation may lawfully show prospects properties listed with other firms. If prospects have not agreed to contractual buyer representation, they are free to walk away and later buy any or all property they have been shown by the first firm through another firm.

This is true when the affiliate has continued in the role of presumed buyer representative. It is also true when prospects are being assisted by an affiliate who has refused implied buyer representation and is serving as the intra-company agent of sellers. Either instance could give rise to disputes between firms about *procuring cause*.

Brokers should carefully reexamine and, where necessary, revise their policy and procedure manuals, office Standard Operating Procedures and all representation agreement forms to take into account the categories of representation in the present law including, of course, presumed buyer representation.

CONFIDENTIALITY

Whatever confidential information a licensee learns from individuals while representing them—either by agreement or as presumed buyer representatives—such as information about their personal finances, bargaining strategy and motivations to buy or to sell must, of course, be kept confidential throughout the conduct of the transaction. This is true even if the prospect rejects representation and chooses customer-level service. Moreover, the confidentiality continues even after the transaction is terminated or completed and after the formal agency agreement has expired.

Agents are forbidden to reveal confidential information to other clients whom they may later represent—or to other agents in their own company who may represent

parties negotiating with the previous clients —or to use such "inside information" to the disadvantage of the previous clients. They must even disclose this restriction on their ability to reveal any such facts to any new client whom they come to represent in dealings with their "old" client. This may require repeated and emphatic retraining in companies where talking about cases, clients and customers was customary.

It is necessary for brokerage offices to provide locked files, or other security arrangements, so that confidential information about buyers or sellers in the same transaction can be kept segregated and not fall into the hands of the intra-company agent representing the wrong party. The broker has full access to all this information but may not, by law, share it with adverse parties in any transaction unless required to by court order or the demands of disclosure of material facts.

AGENCY RELATIONSHIP AND PAYMENT OF FEES

Maryland law clearly states that agency relationships and responsibilities are not determined by which party pays for brokerage services. A seller may pay part or all of the brokerage fee charged by a licensee representing a buyer without becoming the client of that licensee. Moreover, it is not necessary for a brokerage fee to be promised or paid to create an agency relationship.

Certain behaviors and statements of a licensee, however, may be construed (interpreted) by a member of the public—and later, a jury—to indicate that the licensee is indeed their agent, even when no such agreement has been entered into between them. For instance, a licensee who says to a customer, "Trust me; I'll get you a great deal," has asked the customer to regard him as trustworthy and loyal—i.e., as an agent. If this occurs when the licensee is already serving as agent or sub-agent for the sellers in the same transaction, an undisclosed (and probably unintended) dual agency is created that may later prove to be the basis for rescission of sales contract, loss of commission, suit for damages and disciplinary action by the Commission.

No individual licensee can *directly* and *personally* represent both parties to a residential transaction. The broker of a company properly involved in a dual agency situation is a *dual agent*, but does not directly and personally deal with the parties: the broker appoints intra-company agents to do so.

Because of the need to have two affiliates to take these assignments, a firm consisting of a broker and only one affiliate may not perform dual agency under Maryland law.

AGENCY DISCLOSURE

According to the Code of Ethics and the Regulations of the Commission, the obligation of absolute fidelity to the client's interest is primary, but it does not relieve licensees from the obligation to deal fairly with all parties to a transaction.

The Brokers Act requires all licensees who are representing sellers to disclose to buyers or their agents the fact that they are representing sellers. When they represent buyers, they are similarly required to

disclose that fact to sellers. This disclosure must be made *at the first scheduled face-to-face meeting* with such parties.

The Commission's agency relationship information form, mandated in prior years for similar disclosures, is presented in Figure 4/5.1. Students are urged to check with their teacher, a local real estate board, or the Commission to ensure that they have the most up-to-date form. It will also be available through the Commissions's home page.

ORGANIZATION OF BROKERAGE FIRMS: PRACTICE THROUGH CORPORATIONS, PARTNERSHIPS OR LIMITED LIABILITY COMPANIES

To qualify to provide real estate brokerage services through a corporation, partnership or limited liability company, a licensed real estate broker must be employed by or have another contractual relationship with such entity, have been designated by the entity as the broker of the firm individually responsible for the provision of real estate brokerage services through it and submit notice to the Commission stating the broker's intention to do so. The notice must include the name of the real estate broker submitting the notice, a statement that the named individual has been designated as the broker of the firm, the address of the firm's principal place of business and of each proposed branch office, any trade or fictitious name that the firm intends to use while conducting the business of the firm, a list of all the licensed associate real estate brokers and licensed real estate salespersons who will be affiliated with the broker of the firm and any other information that the Commission may require by regulation. The Commission maintains current information regarding any corporation or partnership through which real estate brokerage services are provided.

An individual who provides brokerage services for a firm while associated with the firm as a partner, officer, shareholder or in any other capacity must hold either a salesperson's or an associate broker's license. Company officers, shareholders, etc., who do not provide brokerage services need not be licensed. Individuals who serve as brokers of firms are responsible for the provision of real estate brokerage services through those firms and are subject to all of the provisions of the Brokers Act regarding those services.

A corporation, partnership or limited liability company that provides real estate brokerage services is not, by its compliance with the requirements for so doing, relieved of any responsibility that it may have for any acts or omissions of its officers, partners, employees or agents. An individual who provides real estate brokerage services through a corporation or partnership is not, by reason of employment or other relationship with the corporation, partnership or limited liability company, relieved of any individual responsibility regarding those services.

LIMITATION ON INTERESTS HELD BY AFFILIATES

Not more than 50 percent of ownership control in any form of business organization providing real estate brokerage services may be held directly or indirectly by salespersons or associate brokers or any

combination thereof. Any percentage holding of such ownership by an unlicensed immediate family member of a licensee shall be considered as being held by that licensee for purposes of this 50-percent limitation.

EMPLOYMENT OF AND CONTRACTUAL ARRANGEMENTS WITH SALESPERSONS AND ASSOCIATE BROKERS

Brokers may provide brokerage services only personally or through real estate salespersons or associate brokers licensed under them. Such affiliates typically act as independent contractors or as employees. Any individual, including a licensed associate real estate broker, who provides real estate services on behalf of a real estate broker shall be considered a real estate salesperson with respect to the provision of those services.

SUPERVISION

Real estate brokers are required to exercise reasonable and adequate supervision over the provision of real estate brokerage services by any individuals on their behalf. This requirement applies regardless of whether the individuals are independent contractors or employees. The exercise of reasonable and adequate supervision over the activities of the brokers' salespersons is not construed or deemed to create an employer/employee relationship between the brokers and licensed salespersons under the brokers' supervision. Such supervision requires brokers to direct and review the professional activities of all licensees in the company including branch office managers. Branch office managers are expected to direct and review all activities of licensees in their branch offices.

"Reasonable and adequate" supervision includes provision of regular training and/or education sessions and the review by experienced supervisory personnel of contract provisions, listing provisions and advertising. Written company and office policies and procedures should be in place concerning handling deposits and similar monies. There must also be established procedures for communicating new or changed requirements in federal, state and local real estate related laws and regulations to all affiliated with a company.

When judging whether supervision has been sufficient, the Commission will take into account the number of licensees affiliated with the broker, the number of branch offices and similar variables.

PERSONAL ASSISTANTS

Some salespersons and associate brokers have been using personal assistants to help them in the conduct of their work. Some of these assistants hold real estate licenses, while others do not.

A 1994 memorandum from the Commission states, in pertinent part,

> . . . licensees should be extremely careful in delegating responsibilities to others. They should also be aware that, under the Internal Revenue Code, a person whom they hired to assist them would most likely be considered an employee of the licensee who retained him or her and the licensee would be liable for complying with all IRS requirements on record keeping and payroll deduction, as well as being

responsible for carrying workmen's compensation insurance.

Referring to those acting as personal assistants, the publication continues:

> . . . [U]nlicensed persons, *as well as licensed agents employed by associate brokers or salespersons* [emphasis added] may not provide real estate brokerage services.

It urges seeking legal counsel for specific situations.

What Personal Assistants May and May Not Do

The Commission's guidelines list acts that personal assistants may and may not perform. Note that the word *licensee* as it appears in the guidelines means a licensed associate broker or salesperson affiliated with and acting under the supervision of a broker.

A personal assistant may:

- Answer the telephone and forward calls to a licensee.
- Submit listings and changes to a multiple listing service.
- Follow up on loan commitments after a contract has been negotiated.
- Assemble documents for closing.
- Secure documents (public information) from courthouse, public utilities, etc.
- Have keys made for company listings.
- Write ads for approval of licensee and supervising broker and place advertising.
- Type contract forms at the direction of and for approval by licensee and supervising broker.
- Compute commission checks.
- Place signs on property.

- Type contract forms at the direction of and for approval by licensee and supervising broker.
- Compute commission checks.
- Place signs on property.
- Arrange the date and time of home inspection, termite inspection, mortgage application, well or septic inspection, pre-settlement walk-through or settlement.
- Prepare flyers and promotional information for approval by licensee and supervising broker.
- Act as courier service to deliver documents, pick up keys, etc.
- Schedule an open house.
- Schedule appointments for licensee to show listed property.
- Accompany a licensee to an open house or showing:
  1. for security purposes;
  2. to hand out preprinted materials.

A personal assistant may not:

- Prepare promotional materials or ads without the review and approval of licensee and supervising broker.
- Show property.
- Answer any questions on listings, title, financing, closing, etc.
- Discuss or explain a contract, listing, lease, agreement, or other real estate document with anyone outside the brokerage.
- Be paid on the basis of real estate activity, such as a percentage of commission, or any amount based on listings, sales, etc.
- Negotiate or agree to any commission, split, management fee or referral fee on behalf of a licensee.
- Solicit property owners to list their property for sale, either in person or by telephone.
- Solicit purchasers or lessees for the purchase or lease of real property.

- Discuss with prospective purchasers or lessees the attributes or amenities of a property, whether at an open house or under any other circumstances.
- Discuss with the owner of real property the terms and conditions of the real property offered for sale or lease.
- Collect, receive or hold deposit monies, rent, other monies or anything else of value received from the owner of the real property or from a prospective purchaser or lessee.
- Provide owners of real property or prospective purchasers or lessees with any advice, recommendations or suggestions as to the sale, purchase, exchange or leasing of the real property to be listed or real property presently available for sale or for lease.
- Hold himself or herself out in any manner, orally or in writing, as being licensed or affiliated with a particular company or real estate broker as a licensee.

WORKER'S COMPENSATION

Some real estate salespersons and associate real estate brokers may be exempt from the worker's compensation requirements if they are on a commission-only basis under a written agreement with the broker and otherwise qualified as independent contractors for federal tax purposes. The IRS has set forth guidelines for *independent contractor* status. Companies should seek the advice of competent counsel in this matter.

SALES COMMISSION DISPUTES

The licensing law does not provide for the Real Estate Commission to arbitrate disputes between brokers or between brokers and salespersons as to distribution of commissions. Such disputes should be submitted for arbitration to the respective Board or Association of REALTORS® if the parties to the dispute are members of the same board or to the Maryland Association of REALTORS® if the parties to the dispute are members of different boards or associations. Arbitration may be pursued through other agencies. To prevent commission disputes, the percentage and distribution of commissions should be in writing, especially those setting forth the agreement between brokers and their salespersons.

PLACES OF BUSINESS—OFFICES

Each licensed real estate broker who is a nonresident of the State shall also maintain an office in Maryland if the state in which the nonresident broker resides requires a resident of this State who is licensed in the other state to maintain an office in that state.

The place of business in Maryland required by this Act for all broker licensees must be an office or headquarters where they and their employees and/or affiliates regularly transact real estate business. Records of the brokerage's transactions, including the records of the broker's escrow account, must be kept in a secured location at this office. A commercial answering service, a mechanical recording device or a mail drop, singly or in combination, do not meet the requirements for an office. Brokers must display in their main offices their own licenses and the licenses of all their affiliates who work at that location.

The *Americans with Disabilities Act* requires places of public accommodation to make reasonable modifications to meet the needs of handicapped members of the public. Real estate offices are such places. Access for the public should be barrier free and employees alerted to assist any challenged persons who visit an office. Moreover, every firm with 15 or more employees—and this includes affiliates—must make reasonable accommodation to the needs of any handicapped person working for the firm.

Office Signs

A real estate broker must display a sign clearly visible to the public at each office and branch office that the real estate broker maintains, which sign must include the words *Realty, Real Estate* or, where authorized by the respective trade associations, *REALTOR®* or *Realtist*.

Change in Location of Offices

Within ten days of changing the location of any office, a real estate broker must submit written notice on a form provided by the Commission of such change in the address of the principal office or any branch office of the broker; the license certificate and pocket card of the broker or, for the branch office, its certificate; and the required fee. Upon receipt of these things the Commission shall issue a new certificate and card to the broker for the unexpired period of the broker's license or branch office certificate. If a real estate broker changes the address of the principal office or a branch office of the broker and fails to submit the required notice, the license of the broker is automatically suspended until the broker submits the required notice.

their branch office. This responsibility is in addition to, and not in lieu of, the responsibility of the broker. Licenses of all licensees working out of a branch office are displayed in that branch office together with a branch office certificate that shows, among other things, the name of the broker as registered with the Commission and the address of the main office.

Branch office certificates renewed in early 1998 were given staggered expiration dates. Upon their next renewal, they will be good for a two-year period. Newly issued certificates—as contrasted with renewals—are for a two-year period. There is a $5 fee for each certificate. Applications for branch office certificates must identify the individuals appointed as managers of the branch offices and be accompanied by payment of the required fees.

ADVERTISING

Both the Brokers Act and COMAR require all licensees to show in all advertising the fact that they are licensees. This disclosure must be made even when the licensees are selling their own real property. Licensees affiliated with a broker who use their own names and/or phone numbers in advertisements must clearly identify the broker under whom they are licensed. Even unintentional or careless violations of this requirement may result in a reprimand, suspension, loss of license and/or fine. Licensees may advertise only those properties for which their brokerage is the listing company.

Licensees using a *trade name* (for example, the name of a franchise) on a "for sale" sign, business card, office sign, sales contract, listing contract or other document are required to clearly and unmistakably include their own name or trade name as registered with the Commission. The same rule applies to telephonic and to face-to-face conversations: the broker's name as registered with the Commission must be made clear in each encounter.

A broker's outdoor advertisements or "for sale" signs posted on any property that is subject to *ground lease* must state the annual ground rent and capitalization if the price of the leasehold property is shown on the sign. The capitalization is the sum for which the property could be purchased *in fee*. The lettering showing the ground rent and capitalization must be at least as large as the lettering showing the property sale price. Maryland ground rents are discussed in Chapter 16 of this volume.

COMAR requires that a licensee obtain an owner's permission before placing signs on a property. Licensees should check local laws regarding the use of "for sale," directional and open house signs on public property. They should also honor any restrictions imposed by cooperatives, condominiums and homeowner associations. Licensees should familiarize themselves with HUD guidelines and rules concerning the use of the Equal Housing Opportunity logo or slogan to avoid giving even the appearance of discriminatory practices.

FUNDS OF OTHERS HELD IN TRUST

Trust money is defined as a deposit, payment or other money that a person entrusts to a real estate broker to hold for the benefit of the owner or beneficial owner of that money and for a purpose that relates to a transaction involving real estate in this State.

concerning the use of the Equal Housing Opportunity logo or slogan to avoid giving even the appearance of discriminatory practices.

FUNDS OF OTHERS HELD IN TRUST

Trust money is defined as a deposit, payment or other money that a person entrusts to a real estate broker to hold for the benefit of the owner or beneficial owner of that money and for a purpose that relates to a transaction involving real estate in this State.

The *beneficial owner* of funds in a trust account is that person, other than the owner (source) of the trust money, for whose benefit a licensee holds the money. For instance, the owner of an earnest money deposit is the purchaser while the beneficial owner is the seller.

Handling of Trust Money

Associate real estate brokers or real estate salespersons who obtain trust money while providing real estate brokerage services shall promptly submit that money to the broker they are representing.

Unless real estate brokers receive written directions to the contrary, they must promptly deposit trust money into accounts separate from their own funds and used solely for trust money. Real estate brokers may not use trust money for any purpose other than that for which it is entrusted to them. Unless directed in writing to the contrary by the owner and the beneficial owner, brokers must place trust money in non-interest-bearing checking accounts, non-interest-bearing savings accounts, or any combination of these accounts.

Authorized Financial Institution

Except when directed to the contrary brokers must deposit all trust money in a financial institution located in the State whose deposits are insured by the Federal Deposit Insurance Corporation, the Federal Savings and Loan Insurance Corporation, the National Credit Union Administration, the State of Maryland Deposit Insurance Fund Corporation or the Maryland Credit Union Insurance Corporation.

Maintenance and Disposition of Trust Money

A real estate broker shall maintain trust money in an authorized account until

- the real estate transaction for which the trust money was entrusted is consummated or terminated;
- the real estate broker receives proper written instructions from the owner and beneficial owner directing withdrawal or other disposition of the trust money; or
- on an interpleader filed by the real estate broker, a court orders a different disposition.

When the duty of real estate brokers to maintain trust money in an account terminates, they must promptly account for all trust money.

Real estate brokers may invest trust money as the owners and beneficial owners of the trust money instruct in writing or as the real estate brokers, owners and beneficial owners make written agreement.

In October 1986, at the request of the Talbot County Board of REALTORS®, the Commission agreed to a procedure widely practiced throughout the State by many brokers, whereby language is contained in the sales contracts authorizing the broker to withhold depositing the trust money funds in escrow accounts until the seller executes and accepts the contract.

Brokers are required to report the bank's name and account number to the Commission as soon as any trust monies are received. If a licensee establishes another non-interest-bearing or special escrow account, changes the escrow account number or transfers the account to another bank, the broker must notify the Commission in writing within ten days after the action.

Licensees must maintain, in a secured area within their office, adequate records of all real estate transactions engaged in by them as licensees. The records of transactions, including bank accounts or deposits referred to in these regulations, are to be available during usual business hours for inspection by the Commission, its field representatives or other employees.

The real estate broker must be signer, or at least one of the signers, on checks drawn on escrow accounts that the broker is required to maintain. The broker may designate an alternate signer to sign checks. This designated alternate signer, however, must be a licensee. A non-licensee may be a cosigner on the broker's escrow account, provided all checks are also signed by a designated licensee.

QUESTIONS

1. Any outdoor sign or advertisement displayed on property for sale subject to ground rent

   a. must, if price is shown, also show the annual ground rent but need not show any other details until inquiry is made by a prospective purchaser.
   b. must, if price is shown, show ground rent and cost of capitalization in lettering no smaller than the lettering used for the price.
   c. need show only leasehold price.
   d. need show only leasehold price and the phrase *plus GR*.

2. When licensees advertise real property they have listed for sale

   a. the name of the salesperson may not be included in the advertisement unless the identity of the broker is also included.
   b. only the broker's name is permitted in advertisements.
   c. the price of the property must be included in all advertisements.
   d. members of multiple-listing services may advertise any of the services' listings.

3.   Real estate brokers in Maryland cannot operate their firms as

  a.   single agency companies representing only the buyers in a transaction.
  b.   single agency companies representing only the sellers in a transaction.
  c.   single agency companies representing both buyers and sellers in the same transactions.
  d.   dual agency companies representing both buyers and sellers in a transaction.

4.   Which of the following statements pertaining to Maryland real estate licenses is NOT correct?

  a.   Their holders are regulated by authority of the *Business Occupations and Professions Article* of the Maryland Annotated Code.
  b.   They are issued and administered by the State Real Estate Commission.
  c.   They are not issued to corporations or associations.
  d.   They are required for every person who sells real estate for consideration.

5.   Salespersons may use their own names and phone numbers in advertising listed property if

  a.   their broker affiliation is clearly shown.
  b.   their office manager's name is shown in letters at least half the size of the salespersons'.
  c.   different colors for the broker's and salespersons' names are used.
  d.   the broker gives permission.

6.   Real estate brokers' principals are their

  a.   managers.
  b.   clients.
  c.   prospects.
  d.   customers.

7.   The designated place of business for a real estate broker's office required by law may properly be a

  a.   telephone answering service.
  b.   post office box.
  c.   van or recreational vehicle registered with the Motor Vehicle Administration.
  d.   definite office location.

8.   In handling a real estate transaction involving the sale of real property a real estate broker

  a.   is always employed by the owner of the property being sold.
  b.   may not act as the agent of the buyer.
  c.   may never represent both buyer and seller in the same real estate transaction without disclosing this fact to both parties in the way required by license law.
  d.   may never represent both buyer and seller.

9.   A real estate brokerage firm performing activities for which a real estate license is required may be operated by

  a.   real estate salespersons.
  b.   an associate broker.
  c.   any person holding a valid real estate license issued by the State Real Estate Commission.
  d.   a licensed real estate broker.

10. Advertising by a broker must include the

    a. trade name of that broker as registered with the Commission.
    b. name of the broker's REALTOR® board or association or Realtist organization.
    c. name of the licensed real estate broker.
    d. name of the licensee who listed the property.

11. Arlene has been assigned by her broker, Marie, to work with Tony to provide buyer representation for the purchase of a property listed by Charise, a salesperson with her company. Marie has named Charise to represent the seller. In this situation which of the following is true?

    a. Tony is a prospect; Arlene is his intra-company agent; Marie is a single agency broker; Charise is the intra-company agent for the seller.
    b. Tony is a client; Arlene is his intra-company agent; Marie is a disclosed dual agent; Charise is the intra-company agent of the purchaser.
    c. Tony is a customer; Arlene is his salesperson; Marie is an intra-company agent; Charise represents the seller.
    d. Tony is a client; Arlene is his intra-company agent; Marie is not a single agency broker; Charise is the intra-company agent for the seller.

12. In Maryland, a residential listing agreement

    a. does not create an agency.
    b. may be oral.
    c. must be in writing.
    d. need not contain a definite termination date.

13. Which of the following statements is true concerning *presumed buyer representation*?

    a. Presumed buyer representation begins when a licensee shows a prospective purchaser a property listed by another brokerage firm.
    b. Presumed buyer representation ends when a licensee shows a prospective purchaser a property listed with another brokerage firm.
    c. A prospective purchaser who declines to enter into a buyer representation agreement is no longer owed confidentiality for matters discussed with the licensee who had been providing presumed buyer representation up to that point.
    d. A licensee is no longer the presumed buyer representative of a purchaser who makes an offer on a property.

14. To deliver real estate brokerage services, a licensed real estate salesperson must

    a. be associated with a licensed real estate associate broker.
    b. perform real estate acts only on behalf of a licensed broker.
    c. be associated with a REALTOR®.
    d. operate a real estate business under his or her own name or trade name.

15. Brokers who represent buyers of real estate

    a. are regarded by the law as dual agents in such transactions.
    b. must disclose this agency relationship to sellers.
    c. are in violation of the Brokers Act.
    d. will not be compensated.

6

Listing Agreements

OVERVIEW

Maryland recognizes brokerage agreements between broker licensees and buyers and between broker licensees and sellers.

Brokerage agreements to represent sellers are called *listings*. Listings may be either open, exclusive-agency or exclusive-right-to-sell agreements. These agency agreements, as described in the principal text, are contracts between brokers and property owners.

CONTENT OF RESIDENTIAL BROKERAGE AGREEMENTS

Although there is no standard form provided by either statute or regulation either for listing contracts or for buyer representation agreements, the law has some specific requirements and prohibitions. For example, all residential listings, whether open or exclusive, must be in writing, be signed by the parties to the agreement and state a definite date upon which the agreement will end without further notice from either party. These contracts must also contain provision for cancellation of the brokerage

relationship by either the client or the broker.

Listings must also show the duties and obligations of the agent and explain the events or conditions that will entitle the agent to commission or other compensation. They must set forth the amount of such compensation and whether agents are authorized to receive compensation from persons other than the clients. They must further state whether agents are authorized to cooperate with other brokers and share compensation with them. They must also reveal the amount of the shared compensation. The parties to a listing may not waive any of the above requirements.

Listings may not take the form of a "net" agreements under which brokers retain all amounts in excess of minimum sales prices.

EFFECTS OF SILENCE

The Brokers Act states that when there is no express agreement to the contrary in the brokerage agreement, listing brokers are **not** required to seek additional offers when the listed property becomes subject to a contract of sale. By contrast, the law states that when there is no agreement to the contrary, brokers **are** required to present additional offers and counteroffers to the sellers of property already subject to such a contract. The distinction is important: in the first case it requires brokers to **seek** offers; in the second, it requires them to **present** offers that are made, typically through other firms, after a property is "sold" (under contract).

OTHER PROVISIONS

Many firms have chosen to incorporate in their listing forms authorization from sellers to perform ministerial acts on behalf of third parties. The law states that when such permission is given, brokers' ministerial acts for nonclients cannot be construed (interpreted) to be in violation of loyalty to their clients. Such a declaration similarly prevents nonclients from claiming client status based upon ministerial acts performed for them by the broker.

Licensees must give copies of the listing agreements to sellers before advertising, showing or offering the listed property. Licensees must also keep copies of all listings indefinitely.

At the time of listing a property for sale, brokers are to present the Residential Property Disclosure and Disclaimer Statement to sellers for their completion and signature.

In most listing forms, sellers are also given choices with respect to dealing with buyer agents, subagents and dual agents. These choices are indicated on the completed listing forms together with such

routine issues as offering price, date of availability, acceptable forms of financing and help with purchasers' closing costs.

ADDITIONAL RESPONSIBILITIES

Licensees representing either a seller or a buyer must, at the first scheduled face-to-face meeting with the opposing party, give that party the Agency Relationship Information Form mandated by the Commission, which discloses their fiduciary position. See Figure 4/5.1 in Chapter 4/5 of this volume.

Most brokers have a policy of providing all prospective buyers of a listed property with a copy of the Property Condition Disclosure and Disclaimer Statement at the time of showing a listed property. See Figure 6.1. They also provide the federal lead paint disclosure form for property under consideration built prior to 1978.

Failure to provide required disclosures may enable buyers to rescind contracts. Maryland Real Estate Commission regulations state that creating such potential situations by failing to present disclosure forms is a breach of fiduciary duty for which a licensee can be disciplined.

PROPERTY INFORMATION

The age of the house, area of the lot, zoning of the property, taxes and other detailed property information should appear in the portion of listing agreements that will be published. If accurate data are not available from the owner, the listing licensee should obtain correct data from public records or personal inspection.

Figure 6.1 Property Disclosure and Disclaimer Statement (Page 1 of 4)

MARYLAND RESIDENTIAL PROPERTY DISCLOSURE AND DISCLAIMER STATEMENT

Property Address: _____

Legal Description: _____

NOTICE TO SELLER AND PURCHASER

Section 10-702 of the Real Property Article, Annotated Code of Maryland, requires the owner of certain residential real property to furnish to the purchaser either (a) a RESIDENTIAL PROPERTY DISCLAIMER STATEMENT stating that the owner is selling the property "as is" and makes no representations or warranties as to the condition of the property or any improvements on the real property, except as otherwise provided in the contract of sale, or (b) a RESIDENTIAL PROPERTY DISCLOSURE STATEMENT disclosing defects or other information about the condition of the real property actually known by the owner, Certain transfers of residential property are excluded from this requirement (see the exemptions listed below).

10-702. EXEMPTIONS. - The following are specifically <u>excluded</u> from the provisions of Sections 10-702:
1. The initial sale of single family residential real property:
       A. that has never been occupied, or
       B. for which a certificate of occupancy has been issued within 1 year before the seller and buyer enter a contract of sale.

2. A transfer that is exempt from the transfer tax under §13-207 of the Tax-Property Article, except land installmer contacts of sale under §13-207(11) of the Tax-Property Article and options to purchase real property under §13-2(of the Tax-Property Article;

3. A sale by a lender, or an affiliate or subsidiary of a lender, that acquired the real property by foreclosure or dee lieu of foreclosure.

4. A sheriff's sale, tax sale, or sale by foreclosure, partition, or by court appointed trustee;

5. A transfer by a fiduciary in the course of the administration of a decedent's estate, guardianship, conservatorsh trust; or

6. A transfer of single family Residential Real Property to be converted by the buyer into use other than residenti: or to be demolished.

7. A sale of unimproved real property.

MARYLAND RESIDENTIAL PROPERTY DISCLOSURE STATEMENT

NOTICE TO OWNERS: Complete and sign this statement only if you elect to disclose defects or other information about the condition of the property actually known by you; otherwise, sign the Residential Property Disclaimer Statement. You may wish to obtain professional advice or inspections of the property; however, you are not required to undertake or provide any independent investigation or inspection of the property in order to make the disclosure set forth below. The disclosure is based on your personal knowledge of the condition of the property at the time of the signing of this statement.

NOTICE TO PURCHASERS: The information provided is the representation of the Owners and is based upon the actual knowledge of Owners as of the date noted. Disclosure by the Owners is not a substitute for an inspection by an independent home inspection company, and you may wish to obtain such an inspection. The information contained in this statement is not a warranty by the Owners as to the condition of the property of which the Owners have no knowledge or other conditions of which the Owners have no actual knowledge.

How long have you owned the property? _____

Property System:	Water, Sewage, Heating & Air Conditioning (Answer all that apply)				
Water Supply	❏ Public	❏ Well	❏ Other ____		
Sewage Disposal	❏ Public	❏ Septic System approved for ____ (# bedrooms)			
Garbage Disposal	❏ Yes	❏ No			
Dishwasher	❏ Yes	❏ No			
Heating	❏ Oil	❏ Natural Gas	❏ Electric	❏ Heat Pump Age _____	❏ Other_____
Air Conditioning	❏ Oil	❏ Natural Gas	❏ Electric	❏ Heat Pump Age _____	❏ Other_____
Hot Water	❏ Oil	❏ Natural Gas	❏ Electric Capacity _____ Age_____		❏ Other_____

FORM: DLLR/REC/P/#10/10-95/MMD/96-218

Figure 6.1   Property Disclosure and Disclaimer Statement (Page 2 of 4)

Please indicate your actual knowledge with respect to the following:

1. Foundation: Any settlement or other problems: ❑ Yes ❑ No ❑ Unknown
COMMENTS: _____

2. Basement: Any leaks or evidence of moisture? ❑ Yes ❑ No ❑ Unknown ❑ Does Not Apply
COMMENTS: _____

3. Roof: Any leaks or evidence of moisture? ❑ Yes ❑ No ❑ Unknown
   Type of roof: _____ Age: _____
COMMENTS: _____

   Is there any existing fire retardant treated plywood? ❑ Yes ❑ No ❑ Unknown
COMMENTS: _____

4. Other Structural Systems, including Exterior Walls and Floors:
COMMENTS: _____

   Any Defects (structural or otherwise)? ❑ Yes ❑ No ❑ Unknown
COMMENTS: _____

5. Plumbing System: Is the system in operating condition? ❑ Yes ❑ No ❑ Unknown
COMMENTS: _____

6. Heating Systems: Is heat supplied to all finished rooms? ❑ Yes ❑ No ❑ Unknown
COMMENTS: _____

   Is the system in operating condition? ❑ Yes ❑ No ❑ Unknown
COMMENTS: _____

7. Air Conditioning System: Is cooling supplied to all finished rooms? ❑ Yes ❑ No ❑ Unknown ❑ Does Not Apply
COMMENTS: _____

   Is the system in operating condition? ❑ Yes ❑ No ❑ Unknown ❑ Does Not Apply
COMMENTS: _____

8. Electric Systems: Are there any problems with electrical fuses, circuit breakers, outlets or wiring?
❑ Yes ❑ No ❑ Unknown
COMMENTS: _____

9. Septic Systems: Is the septic system functioning properly? ❑ Yes ❑ No ❑ Unknown ❑ Does Not Apply
   When was the system last pumped? Date _____ ❑ Unknown
COMMENTS: _____

10. Water Supply: Any problem with water supply? ❑ Yes ❑ No ❑ Unknown
COMMENTS: _____

    Home Water Treatment system: ❑ Yes ❑ No ❑ Unknown
COMMENTS: _____

    Fire sprinkler system: ❑ Yes ❑ No ❑ Unknown ❑ Does Not Apply
COMMENTS: _____

    Are the systems in operating condition? ❑ Yes ❑ No ❑ Unknown
COMMENTS: _____

11. Insulation:
    In exterior walls? ❑ Yes ❑ No ❑ Unknown
    In ceiling/attic? ❑ Yes ❑ No ❑ Unknown
    In any other areas? ❑ Yes ❑ No Where:
COMMENTS: _____

Figure 6.1 Property Disclosure and Disclaimer Statement (Page 3 of 4)

12. Exterior Drainage: Does water stand on the property for more than 24 hours after a heavy rain?
❑ Yes   ❑ No   ❑ Unknown
COMMENTS: _____

    Are gutters and downspouts in good repair?   ❑ Yes   ❑ No   ❑ Unknown
COMMENTS: _____

13. Wood-destroying insects: Any infestation and/or prior damage: ❑ Yes   ❑ No   ❑ Unknown
COMMENTS: _____

    Any treatments or repairs?   ❑ Yes   ❑ No   ❑ Unknown
    Any warranties?   ❑ Yes   ❑ No   ❑ Unknown
COMMENTS: _____

14. Are there any hazardous or regulated materials (including, but not limited to licensed landfills, asbestos, radon gas, lead based paint, underground storage tanks, or other contamination) on the property?   ❑ Yes   ❑ No   ❑ Unknown
If yes, specify below.
COMMENTS: _____

15. Are there any zoning violations, nonconforming uses, violation of building restrictions or setback requirements or any recorded or unrecorded easement, except for utilities, on or affecting the property?   ❑ Yes   ❑ No   ❑ Unknown
If yes specify below.
COMMENTS: _____

16. Is the property located in a flood zone, conservation area, wetland area, Chesapeake Bay critical area or Desig
District?   ❑ Yes   ❑ No   ❑ Unknown   If yes,
COMMENTS: _____

17. Is the property subject to any restriction imposed by a Home Owners Association or any other type of communit
❑ Yes   ❑ No   ❑ Unknown   If yes, specify below.
COMMENTS: _____

18. Are there any other materials defects affecting the physical condition of the property? ❑ Yes   ❑ No
COMMENTS: _____

NOTE: Owner(s) may wish to disclose the condition of other buildings on the property on a separate RESIDENTIAL DISCLOSURE STATEMENT.
The owner(s) acknowledge having carefully examined this statement, including any comments, and verify that it is co accurate as of the date signed. The owner(s) further acknowledge that they have been informed of their rights and ot under Section 10-702 of the Maryland Real Property Article.

Owner   _____ Date _____

Owner   _____ Date _____

The purchaser(s) acknowledge receipt of a copy of this disclosure statement and further acknowledge that they have been informed of their rights and obligations under Section 10-702 of the Maryland Real Property Article.

Purchaser _____ Date _____

Purchaser _____ Date _____

Figure 6.1   Property Disclosure and Disclaimer Statement (Page 4 of 4)

MARYLAND RESIDENTIAL PROPERTY DISCLAIMER STATEMENT

NOTICE TO OWNER(S): Sign this statement only if you elect to sell the property without representation and warranties as to its condition, except as otherwise provided in the contract of sale; otherwise, complete and sign the RESIDENTIAL PROPERTY DISCLOSURE STATEMENT.

The undersigned owner(s) of the real property described above make no representations or warranties as to the condition of the real property or any improvements thereon, and the purchaser will be receiving the real property "as is," with all defects which may exist, except as otherwise provided in the real estate contract of sale. The owner(s) acknowledge having carefully examined this statement and further acknowledge that they have been informed of their rights and obligations under Section 10-702 of the Maryland Real Property Article.

Owner   _____   Date   _____

Owner   _____   Date   _____

The purchaser(s) acknowledge receipt of a copy of this disclaimer statement and further acknowledge that they have been informed of their rights and obligations under Section 10-702 of the Maryland Real Property Article.

Purchaser _____   Date   _____

Purchaser _____   Date   _____

PAGE 4 OF 4

Listing licensees should also examine any existing house location survey of the property, notice what information it shows regarding property lines and improvements and determine if it is thorough and up to date. Accurate information responsibly presented in the listing reduces chances for confusion and uncertainty when the property is shown and a contract offer prepared.

When describing the condition of the property in remarks distributed through the MLS, licensees must be careful not to say anything that buyers may later consider misrepresentation. Licensees must also take care not to insert information into the MLS that betrays sellers' confidentiality. **This obligation of confidentiality does not extend to material facts.**

MATERIAL FACTS

To prevent error and misrepresentation, the Commission's **Code of Ethics** requires that licensees make reasonable efforts to discover all **material facts** about each property they list. A material fact includes any negative information about a property that is not readily visible to or discoverable by a prudent purchaser and that would tend to discourage such a purchaser from going forward with a purchase. The Brokers Act requires that licensees disclose such information that they know, **or should know**, to each prospective buyer.

A licensee may not be held personally liable for failure to disclose that an owner or occupant of the property is, was or is suspected of being infected with human immunodeficiency virus (HIV) or diag-

nosed with acquired immunodeficiency syndrome (AIDS) or the fact that a homicide, suicide, natural death, accidental death or felony occurred on the property. The Brokers Act declares that these events are not material facts relating to listed properties. Therefore, failure to disclose them is not a basis for disciplinary action by the Commission.

A licensee needs the express permission of sellers to reveal any of these matters to prospective purchasers or their agents, because such disclosure might impede the sale of the listed property. Notice that, even when sellers have given such permission, under the Brokers Act, licensees need not volunteer the information as they would in the case of material facts. In order to meet the requirement of truthfulness, they must answer prospects' questions about these matters when given sellers' permission.

RESIDENTIAL PROPERTY DISCLOSURE AND DISCLAIMER STATEMENT

At the time a listing agreement is prepared and executed, another important document is completed *by the sellers*. This instrument affects all parties to a sales transaction. It is the Residential Property Disclosure and Disclaimer Statement, presented in Figure 6.1. On this form, sellers choose whether to disclose the condition of a large number of physical features of the listed property. If they choose to make such disclosure, a "completed form" is one in which they respond to every inquiry on the Statement, even if only to say "unknown" or "not applicable."

If they choose not to disclose, they complete the portion of the form that makes this refusal and state that they are selling the property "**as is**." Contrary to popular belief, use of the term *as is* does not free the sellers or their agents from the need to make **voluntary disclosure of material facts**.

Either disclosing or disclaiming may be more appropriate under certain market conditions—such as "buyers' market" or "sellers' market"—but licensees should not direct sellers in this choice. They should certainly not suggest use of the disclaimer as a means of withholding material facts. The authors strongly suggest that to avoid assuming unwarranted liability, the licensee not help the sellers complete the Disclosure and Disclaimer Statement. Rather, advise them to seek any guidance needed for this task from legal counsel and/or other technical professionals. The responses are to be the representations of the owners, not the licensee.

Listing agents should obtain from sellers completed Maryland Residential Property Disclosure and Disclaimer Statements at the time of taking listings. Listing licensees must inform sellers of their rights and obligations arising from this form, which is required in sales of residential properties of four or fewer single family units. (There are seven situations in which single-family properties being sold do not require the use of the form. These limited situations are listed on the preprinted Disclosure and Disclaimer Statement.)

When buyers are not represented by an agent, listing licensees working with prospective buyers must inform them of their rights and obligations with respect to the Property Disclosure and Disclaimer Statement. The duty to make such disclosure falls upon cooperating agents when listed properties are sold by other firms. The rights and obligations of all parties are listed right in this form. The Broker Act requires the Commission to prepare this form and require its use by all brokerage firms in this State.

When listing licensees learn that prospective purchasers are planning to make an offer, they must make every effort to provide them with the Disclosure and Disclaimer Statement in a timely manner. This can be done personally or through the buyers' broker. When listing agents do not know in advance that an offer is forthcoming, they should present the completed Disclosure and Disclaimer Statement to the purchasers or their agent immediately when an offer is produced. The purchasers can then reconsider their offer in the light of the Disclosure and Disclaimer Statement. However, if purchasers receive the Disclosure and Disclaimer Statement before or upon entering into the contract, they may not rescind the contract of sale based upon the information contained in the Disclosure and Disclaimer Statement.

Purchasers who do not receive this Disclosure and Disclaimer Statement before they enter into a sales contract retain the right to rescind the contract for five days after they do receive the form, until they apply for a loan or until they occupy the property, whichever is earliest. If purchasers never get a Disclosure and Disclaimer Statement and are never warned by a lender of the loss of their right to rescind, they can **presumably** rescind at any time before settlement or presettlement occupancy.

TERMINATION OF AGREEMENT

The law sets no minimum or maximum time periods for agency agreements. The term of a listing is negotiable between seller and broker. Because listing agreements, like all brokerage agreements, must contain a definite termination date on which the listing will end without further notice from either party, automatic extension provisions violate the intent of this law.

Unless the agency agreement states to the contrary, licensees have no further obligations or duties to clients after termination, expiration or completion of performance of the brokerage relationship except to account for all trust monies and to keep confidential all personal and financial information about the clients or other matters that clients request be kept confidential.

Death of an owner in severalty would normally terminate an agency agreement by operation of law. However, death of one owner, when a married couple has held title as tenants by the entirety, may not necessarily terminate a listing. It is prudent to have the language of a listing form reviewed by a firm's legal counsel in order to clarify whether such an agency agreement will be binding upon a deceased seller's estate.

Licensees may withdraw from representing either buyer- or seller-clients who refuse to consent to disclosed dual agency and to terminate brokerage relationships with them. However the Brokers Act states that dual agents, simply by making required disclosures of the existence of dual agency, have not thereby terminated their brokerage relationships.

In this State a trustee sale, foreclosure sale, tax sale or condemnation proceeding will generally terminate a listing.

COMMISSIONS

Brokers (typically working through licensees affiliated with them) negotiate their compensation with the sellers in each transaction. The amount or rate of commission charged in a transaction is not set by any law, regulation, association or board. Seller and broker negotiate it. To suggest otherwise is a violation of federal and state antitrust laws and can bring severe penalties. Commission splits between and among brokers in cooperating situations are similarly negotiable. Commission schedules within brokerage firms are established by negotiation between the broker and the affiliates licensed under them.

The Brokers Act specifically states that payments or promises to pay compensation to licensees do not determine that brokerage (agency) relationships have been created or exist nor do they create brokerage relationships. Contrary to a long-held notion, *those who pay agents are not made clients of those agents just because of the payment.*

Sellers typically pay brokerage commissions at settlement, using proceeds arising from the settlement. Brokers and homeowners may, however, agree at the time of listing that if settlement does not take place, no commission is due. Maryland law indicates that, unless there is a previous agreement to the contrary, listing brokers have earned their commissions when sellers accept and sign enforceable contracts of sale. Recent court cases have debated the definition of the term *enforceable*.

According to the Brokers Act, persons performing brokerage services may not maintain an action (sue) for commission unless they had authority to provide those services at the time both of offering to perform and of performing the services.

DUAL AGENCY

Licensees procuring a listing should introduce the sellers to the possibility of a potential buyer also being represented by their company. They should explain the concept of "intra-company agents" as outlined in the Brokers Act and seek the sellers' decision as to whether they will accept dual agency. Please review the discussion in Chapter 4/5 of this volume and earlier in this chapter.

BROKER COOPERATION

The Code of Ethics states that brokers shall cooperate with other brokers on property listed exclusively by their firms whenever it is in the interest of the clients. The companies may then share commissions on a previously agreed-upon basis. Negotiations concerning property subject to exclusive listings must be carried on solely through listing brokers.

In the listing interview, the broker must present to sellers the Agency Relationship Disclosure required by the Commission. See Chapter 4/5 of this volume. At that time the sellers should decide what relationship(s) they are authorizing with cooperating real estate firms: cooperation with subagency, cooperation without subagency (which occurs when a prospective purchaser is represented by a buyer broker) or whichever arises. Sellers should understand that licensees from other companies who represent a purchaser will not be representing them. Sellers should decide if and how the commission they pay will be shared with such other company if cooperation without subagency should arise. Many listing forms allow sellers to authorize their broker to cooperate, work with and offer to compensate buyer brokers by sharing part of the brokerage fee.

In the listing information distributed through the multiple-listing services, brokers should show how sellers have decided to respond to their representation options.

SIGNATURES

When all relevant data have been entered into the listing form, all persons who have an ownership interest in the property must sign it. Alternatively, persons who have proper authorization from the owners —such as a properly drafted power of attorney—may sign the listing for them. Competent legal counsel should be consulted in such situations. It is the responsibility of the listing agent to make sure that the signatures of all required parties are on a listing. A listing becomes effective on the date of the last required signature.

When separated or divorcing couples holding title as tenants by the entireties wish to list property, the authors recommend consultation with the attorneys representing the parties.

Because divorced parties may each retain interests, both their signatures likely will be necessary for an enforceable listing.

When sellers are corporations, trustees, guardians of minors or personal representatives, documentation of the authority of persons signing the listing is often required. A licensee faced with such situations is urged to seek competent legal guidance.

MULTIPLE-LISTING SERVICES (MLSs) AND COMMON SOURCE INFORMATION COMPANIES

The Brokers Act states that licensees who make use of common source information companies, such as multiple-listing services, are not considered to be agents of those services or companies simply by virtue of their use of those companies. Licensees who participate in such companies are not thereby considered to be the agents or subagents of any client of another broker by reason of such participation. These information services may not restrict access to their services to licensees based on the size or type of their licenses.

Several Boards and Associations of REALTORS® offer multiple-listing services serving specific geographical areas. Listing contract forms and numerous

addenda are available from local real estate boards, associations and multiple-listing services for the exclusive use of their members. There are often special forms for different types of property such as residential for sale, commercial/industrial for sale or lease, income property, farms, commercial office rental, residential lots, unimproved land, condominiums, cooperatives and business opportunities. Although the brokerage industry has produced statewide standardized forms, licensees should be alert to differences that still exist between the standardized forms and the forms unique to certain brokerage firms.

The word **REALTOR®** and its related logo appear in the printed portion of many MLS listing and other contract forms. Licensees who use any form that bears the name of an organization of which they are not members violate the Brokers Act.

LOCAL REQUIREMENTS

Licensees should make themselves familiar with and conform to county and municipal requirements in areas where they provide real estate services. For instance, Baltimore County zoning regulations require "development plan notice and conveyances" to be provided to any purchaser of a home in any area covered by an approved development plan. In other counties, air traffic patterns are part of the information prospective purchasers must receive. In 1998, Montgomery County greatly restricted the use of signs. That county has established unique, expensive and cumbersome licensing requirements for persons who wish to post any signs in residential areas within that jurisdiction.

OUT-OF-STATE LISTINGS

Maryland licensees are not authorized to show out-of-state property properly listed and advertised in Maryland unless they also have valid licenses issued in the state where the property is located and comply with all laws of that state.

QUESTIONS

1. Broker use of which type of residential listing agreement is illegal in Maryland?

   a. Net
   b. Exclusive-agency
   c. Open
   d. Exclusive-right-to-sell

2. A seller should complete the Property Disclosure and Disclaimer Statement

   a. at settlement.
   b. when an offer is received.
   c. when the property is being listed.
   d. after a sales contract has been entered into.

3. When purchasers receive no property Disclosure and Disclaimer Statement, either before, at, or after entering into a purchase agreement, the

   a. contract is void by action of law after three days.
   b. purchasers may rescind the contract before they apply for a mortgage loan.
   c. contract is voidable by the purchaser for five days.
   d. lender has five days to tell the purchaser of the right to void the agreement.

4. Sellers must receive a copy of their listing agreement

   a. if they request it.
   b. before the broker advertises the property or offers it for sale.
   c. within 15 days after acceptance by the broker.
   d. only when a buyer is found.

5. In order to show a property located in the State of Virginia but which is multiple listed with a Maryland brokerage, a Maryland licensee must

   a. hold a Virginia real estate license.
   b. be a member of Maryland's multiple-listing service.
   c. be a Maryland broker licensee.
   d. hold a multiple-state license certificate.

6. A listing agreement form published by a multiple-listing service may be used by any

   a. broker or salesperson licensed by the Commission.
   b. member of any Board or Association of REALTORS®.
   c. licensed member of the organization that operates that listing system.
   d. licensee.

7. A listing on Maryland residential property

  a. may contain an automatic renewal provision.
  b. may be parol.
  c. must be in writing and signed by all parties.
  d. may leave the commission fee to be negotiated at the time an offer is made.

8. Purchasers who receive the residential Disclosure and Disclaimer Statement before signing their contract offer may

  a. rescind the contract at any time up to three days after signing.
  b. rescind the contract at any time up to five days after signing.
  c. rescind at any time prior to settlement or to taking occupancy.
  d. not rescind the contract based on any facts the statement discloses.

9. Which statement concerning agency is true?

  a. A broker is the agent of the party who is paying for his services.
  b. A broker is allowed to be a dual agent in a transaction if no harm is done.
  c. A salesperson may personally act as dual agent if both buyer and seller agree in writing.
  d. A broker who represents both buyer and seller in the same transaction must appoint two intra-company agents.

10. The amount or rate of commission on a real estate sale

  a. must be stated in the listing agreement.
  b. is established by the Commission.
  c. is established by the local real estate Board or Association of REALTORS®.
  d. is established by law.

7

Interests in Real Estate

OVERVIEW

Freeholds in fee simple absolute, fee simple determinable, fee simple conditional and life estates—as well as future interests such as remainder and reversion—are recognized in Maryland. Leasehold estates for years, from period to period, at will and at sufferance are also recognized. In addition, a ground rent system, as described in Chapter 16 of this volume, exists in some areas. Concerning legal life estates, both dower and curtesy have been abolished and there is no homestead exemption in Maryland.

EASEMENT BY PRESCRIPTION AND ADVERSE POSSESSION

An easement by prescription may be acquired in Maryland by an adverse user of another's land for a continuous period of 20 years. Similarly, adverse possession can ripen into ownership after 20 years, subject to certain conditions. Consult competent legal counsel in cases involving these matters.

RIPARIAN RIGHTS

Owners of real estate bordering a navigable body of water in Maryland have the common-law right to make a landing, wharf or pier for their own use or for the use of the public, subject to state and federal rules and regulations. However, regardless of whether the owners' title extends beyond the dry land, the title to land below the mean (average) high-water mark of navigable waters, as well as the waters themselves, belongs to the public. Thus, an owner may legally own only the property up to the mean high-water mark. High-water mark is defined as the highest elevation of water in the course of the usual, regular, periodic ebb and flow of the tide, excluding the advance of waters above that line by winds, storms or floods.

For further information regarding water use, contact the Maryland Cooperative Extension Service, the Maryland Department of Agriculture or the Maryland Water Resources Administration.

AGRICULTURAL LAND PRESERVATION EASEMENT

The Maryland Agricultural Land Preservation Foundation has been established to purchase easements on land in certain areas for the purpose of restricting land to agricultural use. Details are contained in the *Agricultural Article* of the Annotated Code of Maryland. The state is purchasing development rights and is limiting residential subdivision of agricultural land. The purchases are funded in large part by the revenues of the State real estate transfer tax.

QUESTIONS

1. Easements to restrict land to agricultural use may be purchased by the

   a. Maryland Land Development Corporation.
   b. Maryland Department of Assessments & Taxation.
   c. Maryland Agricultural Land Preservation Foundation.
   d. Maryland Environmental Department.

2. Legal title to Maryland real estate may be held in all but which of the following ways?

   a. Fee simple determinable
   b. Leasehold
   c. Fee simple absolute
   d. Life estate

3. The *Environmental Article* and the *Natural Resources Article* of the Annotated Code of Maryland do NOT include the statutory laws governing

   a. soil and forest conservation.
   b. sanitary facilities.
   c. licensing of real estate agents.
   d. waters of the state.

4. A person may acquire an easement by prescription in Maryland land over another person's property

   a. after 20 years' continuous use.
   b. after 25 years' intermittent use.
   c. after 30 years' continuous use.
   d. only if it is an easement by necessity.

5. Which of the following is recognized in Maryland?

   a. Dower
   b. Homestead exemption
   c. Curtesy
   d. Easement by prescription

6. Jefferson Thomas owns several acres of land in Maryland. His property is divided by a navigable river. Thomas has the right to

   a. build a pier on one of the riverbanks, subject to state and federal laws.
   b. construct a dam across the river to divert the waters into a man-made lake on his property.
   c. construct a wharf without state approval.
   d. make use only of the dry land.

8
Forms of Ownership

OVERVIEW

Maryland law recognizes ownership in severalty and various forms of co-ownership—tenancy in common, joint tenancy, tenancy by the entirety, partnership and trust as described in the main text. It also provides for condominium, time-share, and cooperative ownership.

CO-OWNERSHIP

Unless the deed specifies otherwise, a conveyance of Maryland real estate to two or more persons creates a tenancy in common. To create a joint tenancy, it is necessary to use such wording as "to Fred Donaldson and Sam Roberts as joint tenants and not as tenants in common." A deed to a husband and wife is presumed to create a tenancy by the entirety unless it specifies tenancy in common or joint tenancy.

In Maryland, only a legally married husband and wife can own property as tenants by the entirety. (Common-law marriages cannot be established in Maryland but are recognized as valid if established in other jurisdictions that recognize and permit them.) Both husband and wife must sign the deed in order to convey property they hold as tenants by the entirety. Upon divorce or other legal termination of the marriage, they are considered tenants in common, by operation of law. A tenancy by the entirety is terminated by the death of either spouse. The survivor holds the property in severalty.

Although Maryland is not a community property state, the Property Disposition in Divorce and Annulment statute has much the same effect as community property rulings in other states at the time of divorce. In domestic cases the court may prevent a partition proceeding for a period not to exceed three years if the property is occupied as the "family home" by a custodial spouse and any unemancipated children. This situation arises when property ownership has been changed from tenants by the entirety to tenants in common by action of law (as in divorce).

The provisions of the Uniform Partnership Act apply in Maryland. The statute allows a corporation (as well as an individual) to become a member of a partnership.

The real estate investment trust (REIT), a form of unincorporated trust or association, has been recognized in Maryland since 1963. A declaration of trust must be filed that provides, among other things, the total number of shares to be issued, the classification of shares and the date of the annual shareholders' meeting and election of trustees. At least 75 percent of the value of assets must be real property assets, government securities, cash and receivables. Beneficial ownership must be held by 100 or more persons for at least 75 percent of each year. Fifty percent or more of the shares may not be held directly or indirectly by five or fewer shareholders. The procedures for forming a REIT are so complex that the assistance of legal counsel is recommended.

The Maryland Securities Act, found in the *Maryland Corporations and Associations Article,* requires a securities license for persons engaged in the selling of real estate–related securities.

GRANTS OF INTEREST

A person may grant an interest in real property to himself or herself and any other person, as grantees, in life tenancy with or without powers. An interest in property held by a husband and wife in tenancy by the entirety may be granted to either of them. Such transactions require legal guidance.

CONDOMINIUMS

Maryland law has allowed condominium projects since 1963. In 1972, the statute, now named the Condominium Act, was restated and recodified. It is further revised almost every year. Its detailed provisions are contained in Title 11 of the *Real Property Article* of the Annotated Code of Maryland. The following sections merely highlight some features of the Act. Any licensee involved with condominium sales or development should obtain a complete copy of the law or seek competent advice. Persons developing and selling condominiums are considered brokers and are subject to the licensing provisions of the Maryland Real Estate Brokers Act. The Condominium Act is enforced by the Division of Consumer Protection of the Office of the Attorney Generals in matters affecting consumers.

Definitions

A **condominium** is a property subject to a condominium regime (the plan of organization). It is governed by a **council of unit owners,** which is either an incorporated or unincorporated nonstock corporation. Persons who subject their property to the condominium regime established by the Act are called **developers**. A condominium **unit** is a three-dimensional space described in three dimensions in the declaration and on the condominium plat. It includes all improvements within that space except those excluded by the declaration or the master deed.

Common elements are all parts of a condominium other than the units. There are two types. **Limited common elements** are identified in the declaration or on the condominium plat as reserved for the exclusive use of one or more, but less than all, of the unit owners. **General common elements** are all the common elements except the limited common elements. The expenses and profits of the council of unit owners are called **common expenses** and **common profits.**

Establishment

Those who wish to convert their real estate to condominium ownership must expressly declare their intention to do so by recording a declaration, bylaws and the condominium plat. These documents must comply with the requirements stated in the statute. Property is then said to be under a **condominium regime**, and the owners are regarded as its developer. The declaration is indexed on the county records under both the name of the developer and the name of the condominium. The condominium regime must be registered with the Secretary of State before a condominium unit may be sold or offered for sale. The declaration subsequently may be amended within certain limits by the written consent of 80 percent of the unit owners.

Public Offering Statement

A contract for the *initial* sale of a residential condominium unit to a member of the general public is not enforceable by the seller until the purchaser is given a copy of the Public Offering Statement registered with the Secretary of State. Buyers may make written rescission of a purchase contract, without stating any reason, within 15 days after receipt of the Public Offering Statement. They may also rescind that agreement within five days following receipt of any later amendments to the Statement made by the seller. Buyers who rescind within these time limits are entitled to prompt return of all deposits.

These rights of buyers to rescind terminate upon settlement. However, sellers remain liable to buyers for one year for any damages suffered as a result of the sellers' failure to disclose material facts or their making any false or misleading statements. The purchasers' right to rescind or cancel under the Condominium Act may not be waived in the contract of sale.

Conversion of Residential Rental Facility

Before a residential rental facility is subject to a condominium regime, the tenant must be given a notice in the form prescribed by law. This notice is given after registration with the Secretary of State, along with the Public Offering Statement. A tenant may not be required to vacate the premises prior to the expiration of 180 days from the giving of notice, except for breach of the lease. The tenant may terminate the lease without penalty for termination upon at least 30 days' written notice to the landlord after receiving such notice.

Ownership of Unit and Interest in Common Elements

In addition to exclusive ownership of a condominium unit, each unit owner has a right to share a defined percentage of the undivided interest in the common elements of the property. The unit owners' undivided interest in the common elements cannot be partitioned or separated from the unit to which that percentage is assigned. The council of unit owners is made up of all unit owners. It is considered a legal entity even if unincorporated.

Organization: Declaration and Bylaws; Termination

The recorded declaration must contain at least the name by which the condominium is to be identified, including or followed by the phrase "a condominium"; a description of the land and buildings, with a statement of the owners' intent to establish a condominium regime; a general description and number of each unit, its perimeters, location and other identifying data; a general description of the common elements and the units to which their use is restricted initially; the percentage interest appurtenant to each unit; and the number of votes at meetings of the council of unit owners appurtenant to each unit.

The bylaws must express at least the form of administration, whether the council is to be incorporated, whether the council's duties may be delegated to a board of directors or manager and what powers the owners have in their selection and removal; the council's mailing address; the procedure to be followed in council meetings; and the manner of assessing and collecting unit owners' respective shares of the common expenses. Unless a higher percentage is required in the bylaws, the bylaws may be amended by the affirmative vote of unit owners having at least 66⅔ percent of the votes in the council of unit owners.

Unless taken by eminent domain, a condominium regime may be terminated only by agreement of at least 80 percent of the unit owners, or more if so specified in the declaration. Upon termination of the regime, and unless otherwise provided in the deed of termination, the unit owners become tenants in common, with each owning an interest equal to the former percentage interest in the common elements.

Common Expenses, Taxes, Assessments and Liens

Unit owners are responsible for their percentage share of the common expenses of the council of unit owners. Assessments against unit owners for common expenses become liens on the unit when a statement of lien is recorded within two years after the assessment becomes due. This lien may be foreclosed in the same manner as a mortgage or deed of trust if foreclosure is brought within three years of recording the lien.

If the condominium is intended for residential use, the council of unit owners is required to maintain property insurance on common elements and units and comprehensive general liability insurance, including medical, in amounts set by the declaration, master deed or the council.

Each unit is taxed as a separate and distinct entity on the county tax records. A delinquent tax on a specific unit will not affect the title to any other unit on which all taxes and assessments are paid.

Under the Consumer Protection Act of the *Commercial Law Article* of the Annotated Code of Maryland, certain condominium disputes will be investigated by the Division of Consumer Protection of the Office of the Attorney General, which is authorized to administer a program of voluntary mediation of condominium disputes involving unit owners, boards of directors and/or councils of unit owners.

Resale of Unit

A contract for the resale of a unit by a unit owner other than a developer is not enforceable unless the contract of sale contains in conspicuous type a notice in the form specified in the Condominium Act (Section 11-135). The unit owner is required to furnish to the purchaser not later than 15 days prior to the closing (1) a copy of the declaration (other than the plat); (2) the bylaws; (3) the rules or regulations of the condominium; and (4) a certificate containing statements concerning such things as monthly expenses, proposed capital improvements, fees payable by unit owners, financial statements of the condominium and insurance coverage. These contracts should contain the required clauses and disclosures to ensure compliance with the Act. Some local boards and associations make available to their members a "Condominium Contract of Sale" and "Condominium Listing Contract." The contract of sale is voidable by the purchaser for 7 days after the certificate has been provided or until conveyance of the unit has been made, whichever comes first.

TIME-SHARE OWNERSHIP

There are two principal forms of time-sharing: the right-to-use (time-share license) method and the purchase-of-fractional-interest (time-share estate) method. In the right-to-use form, owners of interests in vacation properties, including condominiums, hotels, motels, marinas and boats, may trade their vacation periods and facilities either directly or indirectly through space banks, which are maintained by firms established to help time-sharers swap vacation facilities.

In the time-share estate, widely used in Maryland in the Eastern Shore and western areas, the customers buy fractional interests, for designated time periods, in a resort condominium on a rental (estate for years) or permanent (fee simple) basis. The fee simple buyer receives a deed for a share of the property. Mortgages or deeds of trust are accepted for the unpaid portion of the purchase price. Contracts, settlements and all other matters are similar to purchases of condominium units.

The State Securities Commission requires that anyone offering part ownership or interest in condominiums must disclose the inherent risks of such an investment. Limited-use resort securities must comply with the registration and antifraud requirements of the State Securities Act.

The Time-Sharing Act

The Time-Sharing Act, Title 11A of the *Real Property Article*, provides for the creation, sale, lease, management and termination of time-share interests; registration of certain documents; registration of time-share developers with the Commission; and certain bonding requirements. Certain advertising and promotion practices are prohibited. Developers are required to prepare Public Offering Statements describing time-share projects regulated by the Secretary of State. Certain protections for purchasers are provided, such as sales contract cancellation periods and disclosures of information, warranties and exchange programs. Terms generally relating to time-share interests in real estate are defined. The following sections highlight some main points of the Act. Any licensee involved in time-share sales or development should obtain a complete copy of the Act or seek competent legal advice. Time-share developers and persons selling time-share estates are also subject to the provisions of the License Law.

Creation

Time-shares may be created in any condominium unit in existence before January 1, 1985, unless prohibited by a project instrument. The owners of at least 34 percent of the units may sign and record a land record document within the county of the project's locale, stating an intent to limit time-shares in the project. Thereafter, no person or other entity may become a developer of more than one unit in the project. Property owners in a residential community governed by recorded covenants and restrictions may prohibit time-shares on any property subject to recorded covenants and restrictions by amending them with a vote of the owners by majority requirements of said covenants and restrictions.

Public Offering Statement

Upon or before the signing of a sales contract, the developers—or other owner-sellers—who offers time-shares for their own accounts must deliver to each purchaser a Public Offering Statement. This could apply to real estate licensees selling their own time-shares.

The requirements for disclosure under the Time-Sharing Act differ substantially from those required under the Condominium Act. A time-share owner who is not associated with the developer of a time-share project is exempt from filing and disseminating a Public Offering Statement.

The Time-Sharing Act provides for substantial penalties for persons convicted of providing or disseminating any false or misleading statement or for any omission of material fact in the Public Offering Statement. Real estate licensees are cautioned to read the Public Offering Statement thoroughly and to refrain from selling any units in the time-share project until they are satisfied that the requirements of the Time-Sharing Act have been met.

Conversions

A developer desiring to convert a building more than five years old into a time-share project is required to include an engineer's report in the Public Offering Statement and to give any tenant or subtenant at least 120 days' notice of the intention to convert the building to a time-share project.

Cancellation Rights

Purchasers of time-shares have the right to cancel the sales contract until midnight of the tenth calendar day following whichever occurs latest: (1) the contract date, (2) the day on which the time-share purchaser received the last of all documents required as part of the Public Offering Statement or (3) the date on which the time-share unit meets all building requirements and is ready for occupancy or if the developer obtains a payment and performance bond and files the bond with the Commission. The right of cancellation cannot be waived. No closing can occur until the purchaser's cancellation period has expired. If closing is held prior to the cancellation period, the closing is voidable at the option of the purchaser for a period of one year after the expiration of the cancellation period.

Resale Disclosures

An owner selling his or her time-share is required to furnish to the purchaser before execution of the contract, transfer of title or use (1) a copy of the time-share instrument and (2) a resale certificate containing the information required by the Time-Sharing Act. The purchaser may cancel the contract to purchase at any time within seven days after receipt of the resale certificate without reason and without liability and with the return of any deposits made under the contract.

Deposits

All purchase money received by a developer from a purchaser must be deposited in an escrow account designed solely for that purpose with a financial institution whose accounts are insured by a government agency. The funds remain there until the end of the ten-day cancellation period or any later time provided for in the contract. Purchase money may be released to the developer, provided the developer maintains a surety bond for the benefit of each purchaser. No claim can be made against the Real Estate Guaranty Fund (described in Part I of this volume) if the claim is covered by the surety bond.

Warranties

All time-share units sold by developers have implied warranties of three years for common elements and one year for units with respect to structural components and heating and cooling systems. In addition, the developer must warrant to a purchaser of a time-share that any existing use of the time-share unit that will continue does not violate any law.

Sales Contract

The statute requires contracts for the sale of time-shares to use specific language to disclose cancellation rights. Contracts must also show the estimated completion date of each unit and each common element as well as estimates of the time-share expenses and facility fees. All this is intended to disclose the total financial obligation being incurred by purchasers.

Exchange Programs

The Time-Sharing Act requires detailed information concerning each exchange program a developer makes available for purchasers' use. To comply with the Act, each exchange company offering an exchange program is required to file the required information with the Commission on an annual basis.

Registration

The Time-Sharing Act requires developers, with certain exceptions, to register with the Commission. A developer may not offer a time-share to the public until the developer has received a certificate of registration as a time-share developer. The developer is required to file certain documents and material with the Commission. The Time-Sharing Act gives the Commission the authority to (1) issue regulations and orders consistent with the Act, (2) investigate possible violations of the Act and subpoena witnesses and documents in connection with the investigations, (3) bring suit against violators, (4) order violators to correct conditions resulting from the violation and (5) revoke the registration of any developer who is convicted of violating the Act. In addition, the Secretary of State is authorized to adopt regulations necessary to implement and enforce the provisions of the Act pertaining to Public Offering Statements. A violation of the Act could provide grounds for the suspension or revocation of a broker's or salesperson's license under the Brokers Act.

Project Broker

Developers are required to designate licensed real estate brokers as project brokers for each time-share project. Each time-share project is considered a separate real estate office for purposes of the Real Estate License Law. Any person who sells, advertises or offers for sale any time-share must be a licensed broker, associate broker or salesperson or be exempt from licensure under the license law. An unlicensed person may be employed by a developer or project broker to contact, but not solicit, prospective buyers so long as the unlicensed person (1) performs only clerical tasks, (2) schedules only those appointments induced by others or (3) prepares or distributes only promotional materials.

Penalties and Remedies

Remedies provided by the Time-Sharing Act are intended to compensate aggrieved parties fully. A court, upon finding that a sales contract or a clause in a contract is unconscionable, may refuse to enforce the contract. If a developer or any other person fails to comply with any provisions of the Act, punitive damages may be awarded, along with reasonable attorney's fees. Any purported conveyance, encumbrance, judicial sale, foreclosure sale or other voluntary or involuntary transfer of a time-share made without the use period that is part of that time-share is void. Penalties and remedies provided by the Act are in addition to penalties and remedies available under any other law or regulation.

Time-share Regulations

Regulations governing time-shares (found in COMAR 09.11.04) require that records be maintained of names and addresses of all personnel retained for sale of time-share estates, including agents, employees and licensees whether employees or independent contractors. Records must also be made and kept of all sales transactions, of estates conveyed and encumbrances on them and of amounts of purchase money held for such sales. The Commission may require certification of such amounts by a certified public accountant. Developers must also maintain bonding in prescribed amounts for deposit monies being held.

Statements in connection with time-share marketing relative to the characteristics of the time-share project or estate may not be false, inaccurate or misleading. A developer may not indicate that an improvement will be placed in a time-share project unless the developer has sufficient finances and bona fide intentions to complete the improvement. Statements used in the marketing of time-share estates located in Maryland may not induce a prospective purchaser to leave the State for the purpose of executing a contract for sale when to do so would circumvent the provisions of Maryland law. No one may advertise or represent that the Commission has approved or recommended any time-share project or estate offered for sale.

MARYLAND COOPERATIVE HOUSING CORPORATION ACT

The Maryland Cooperative Housing Act, Title 5-6B of the *Corporations and Associations Article*, Annotated Code of Maryland, provides for conditions, contracts, rights and requirements relative to the development and sale of interests in cooperatives. Detailed provisions are contained in statutes. A member of the cooperative receives a proprietary lease, an agreement with the cooperative housing corporation that gives the member an exclusive possessory interest in a unit and a possessory interest in common with other members in that portion of a cooperative project not constituting units. It creates a legal relationship of landlord and tenant between the corporation and the member.

MARYLAND HOMEOWNERS ASSOCIATION ACT

This Act sets forth conditions, rights and requirements regulating homeowner's associations (HOAs)in the State.

For sales contracts to be binding on purchaser, sellers must make disclosure showing that property is subject to an HOA, and listing the rights, responsibilities and obligations of purchasers.

They must also disclose purchasers' rights of rescission if the Maryland Homeowners Association Act (MHAA) information is not provided to them by sellers in a timely manner. The MHAA information must recite factual details pertaining to disclosures that must be provided to buyers, the amount of HOA fees, the size of the development, exceptions, waiver of rights, government limitations, rescission of contracts, liability, warranties, meetings, books and records.

Time periods for rescission vary with the number of lots in the HOA and between initial sale and resale of properties. See Section 11B in the *Real Property Article*.

NOTICE TO TENANTS— MONTGOMERY COUNTY

In Montgomery County, before execution by a tenant of a lease for an initial term of 125 days or more, the owner of any residential rental property within any condominium or development is required to provide to the prospective tenant—to the extent applicable—a copy of the rules, declaration and recorded covenants and restrictions that limit or affect the use and occupancy of the property or common areas and under which the owner is obligated. The written lease must include a statement, if applicable, that the obligations of the owner that limit or affect the use and occupancy of the property are enforceable against the owner's tenant. Some jurisdictions may make further limitations on sales and leases.

QUESTIONS

1. **All but which** of the following forms of ownership are recognized in Maryland?

   a. Tenancy in common
   b. Community property
   c. Trust
   d. Ownership in severalty

2. In Maryland, a deed that conveys ownership to "Karen and David Maines, husband and wife" but does not specify the form of ownership

   a. automatically creates a tenancy in common.
   b. must be redrawn before the property is sold, specifying the form of ownership.
   c. creates a tenancy by the entirety.
   d. creates an ownership in severalty.

3. Which of the following is NOT true? In Maryland, a tenancy by the entirety

   a. may be held only by a husband and wife.
   b. continues after the death of one of the owners.
   c. gives an individual possession of the entire estate.
   d. may not be partitioned.

4. A time-share developer is required to

   a. register with the State Real Estate Commission.
   b. register with the State Treasurer.
   c. register with the local Board or Association of REALTORS® in the area where the time-share units are located.
   d. be a licensed real estate broker.

5. The bylaws of a condominium can be changed or altered by

   a. the manager of the property.
   b. a two-thirds vote of the unit owners.
   c. the council of unit owners by majority vote.
   d. a simple majority of unit owners.

6. A developer who proposes to convert a residential rental facility to a condominium regime must register with the

   a. office of the Attorney General.
   b. local Board of REALTORS®.
   c. Secretary of State.
   d. Maryland Real Estate Commission.

7. Tenancy by the entirety is for

   a. husbands and wives only.
   b. common-law-marriage spouses.
   c. any family member.
   d. tenants in common.

8. A developer selling a newly built condominium unit to an original purchaser

   a. is liable for damages as a result of misleading statements for five years after the sale.
   b. is subject to the seller's voiding the contract if the developer fails to deliver a Public Offering Statement.
   c. is protected by the doctrine of caveat emptor from liability for misleading statements.
   d. must file a Public Offering Statement with the State Real Estate Commission.

9. Purchasers of time-shares from a developer

    a. have a right to cancel the contract only if the seller has misrepresented material facts.
    b. have ten days in which to cancel the sale for any reason.
    c. must close the sale within ten days after signing the sales contract.
    d. must obtain a payment and performance bond to ensure their compliance with the contract.

10. A contract for sale of a condominium by its owner (other than a developer) is not enforceable unless the owner furnishes the buyer, not later than 15 days prior to the closing,

    a. a copy of the declaration.
    b. the rules and regulations.
    c. a statement regarding monthly expenses, proposed capital improvements, other fees, financial statements of the condominium and insurance details.
    d. All of the above

11. Should a dispute develop between a unit owner, Board of Directors and/or council of unit owners, parties may apply for mediation to the

    a. local Board of REALTORS®.
    b. office of the county state's attorney.
    c. office of the Attorney General.
    d. local Board of Development and Planning.

12. In purchasing a condominium, the most important document to the buyer is the declaration, which in most cases

    a. authorizes a Board of Directors to administer the condominium affairs pursuant to the bylaws and to assess the owners so as to adequately maintain the condominium.
    b. describes the condominium units and the common areas and any restrictions on their use.
    c. establishes the undivided interest percentages.
    d. All of the above

13. The condominium declaration

    a. must be recorded to place the property under a condominium regime.
    b. cannot be rescinded once it is recorded.
    c. can be changed only with the unanimous approval of the council of unit owners.
    d. must be printed in a daily newspaper before changes may be made.

9

Legal Descriptions

OVERVIEW

The **metes and bounds** and **recorded plat of subdivision** methods of property description are used in Maryland. At the very least, a description that identifies land "with reasonable certainty" is required. A postal address alone is usually not an adequate legal description.

EXAMPLES OF LEGAL DESCRIPTIONS USED IN CONTRACTS

- "Beginning at an iron pipe set on the northeast side of Annapolis Street at a point located South 38° 45' East, 200 feet from where the northeast side of Annapolis Street intersects the southeast side of Giddings Avenue—all as shown on Aldridge's Revised and Corrected Plat of West Annapolis recorded among the Land Records of Anne Arundel County in JCB Liber 4, Folio 297; and running thence and at right angles to Annapolis Street, North 51° 15' East, 150 feet to a pipe; thence South 38° 45' East 50 feet to a pipe; thence South 51° 15' West, 150 feet to a pipe on the northeast side of Annapolis Street; thence with same, North 38° 45' West, 50 feet to the place of beginning."

- "That certain parcel of real estate located in Worcester County, Maryland, being on the east side of Farm Lane, north of Jerry Road, being further known as the Arthur R. Jackson property, consisting of one acre, more or less, with the improvements thereon, previously conveyed by deed of Robert Allen, grantor, recorded in FWH Liber 29, Folio 1312, the exact boundaries and acreage to be determined by means of a survey, which has been ordered to be prepared by Johnson and Landsman, surveyors, Snow Hill."

- "Lot #16, Block #3 of the Plat of Melville Development Corporation as surveyed by John Walmer, Catonsville, Maryland, August 15, 1968, as recorded in FWH Liber 295, Folio 1720, in the County of Ridge, State of Maryland."

SURVEY MARKERS

Any person who willfully obliterates, damages or removes any stake, marker, monument or other landmark set in property by any civil engineer, surveyor or real estate appraiser or assistant, except if the marker interferes with the proper use of the property, is guilty of a misdemeanor and on conviction can be fined not more than $500.

If there is a dispute over any boundary line or if the bounds mentioned in a document are lost, the circuit court of the county where the property is located may be petitioned to establish the boundary lines or the location of the missing bounds. The experts' fees are considered costs in the proceeding.

LOCATION DRAWING VS. BOUNDARY SURVEY

The Secretary of Licensing and Regulation, through its Board for Professional Land Surveyors, requires surveyors to have a signed election form requesting either a **location drawing** or a **boundary survey** from the consumer. The boundary survey includes property boundary lines and corners as well as a location drawing. It is used when erecting a fence, building or garage or when making other improvements. The location drawing costs less but is often sufficient for residential resales and refinancing.

A description of each type and of its uses, limitations and costs appears on the election form. Real estate licensees typically supply this form to the purchaser to complete at the time they prepare an offer to purchase.

SUBDIVISION PLATS

Subdividers must have plats of proposed subdivisions prepared by a licensed surveyor and approved and recorded by local authorities before offering them for sale. No distances on a subdivision plat may be marked "more or less" except those lines that begin, terminate or bind on a body of water.

QUESTIONS

1. In Maryland, subdivision plats

   a. are an adequate form of legal description if properly recorded.
   b. must be prepared by licensed real estate brokers.
   c. need not be recorded prior to sale of the lots.
   d. need not have planning and zoning approval prior to recording.

2. A location drawing

   a. is essentially the same as a boundary survey.
   b. is appropriate for typical residential resales.
   c. costs more than a boundary survey.
   d. can properly be used for placing fences and other improvements.

3. Which of the following is most likely to be a sufficient legal description?

   a. 3396 Ocean Pines, 142 Pinehurst Road
   b. That lot fronting on Pinehurst Rd. 100 feet—being 250 feet deep
   c. That two acres, shown on attached survey as prepared by Landsman & Co., surveyors of Catonsville, Maryland
   d. 1776-B Liberty St., Snow Hill, Md., being northern half of duplex

4. "Beginning at the intersection of the east line of Goodrich Boulevard and the south line of Jasmine Lane and running south along the east line of Goodrich Boulevard a distance of 230 feet; thence easterly parallel to the north line of Wolf Road, a distance of 195 feet; thence northeasterly on a course of N 22 E, a distance of 135 feet; and thence northwesterly along the south line of Jasmine Lane to the point of beginning." This legal description is an example of a

   a. block description.
   b. rectangular survey.
   c. subdivision description.
   d. metes and bounds description.

5. Legal descriptions in Maryland

   a. employ the rectangular survey system.
   b. consist of the street or mailing addresses of the properties.
   c. are based on lot and block numbers or metes and bounds data.
   d. consist of the post office box numbers.

10

Real Estate Taxes and Other Liens

OVERVIEW

Maryland property taxes are levied by and for the support of the state, county and city governments, as well as local special taxing districts. A number of counties impose **impact fees** on developers in addition to property taxes on owners. The impact fees are levied on new residential units to fund additional public facilities and services for the use and benefit of new residents.

ASSESSMENT

Real property is assessed for tax purposes by the State Department of Assessments and Taxation. There are local offices of that department in Baltimore City and in each Maryland county.

The procedure for assessing property in Maryland, often called **triennial assessment**, is based on a three-year cycle in which one-third of all properties are revalued every year for tax purposes.

Each county has been organized into three principal assessing areas to coincide with the years of the assessment cycle. The areas generally have similar density and other common characteristics and are reviewed on a rotating basis. By the end of a three-year period, all properties will have been physically reviewed and valued once; then a new cycle commences. An inspection of the exterior premises always accompanies a revaluation. If changes in zoning or use occur, or if additions or extensive improvements to property have been made, the property can be revalued out of sequence.

A real property assessment is further controlled by a **phase-in provision**, designed to take some of the financial sting out of inflation. For the one-third of all real properties reassessed in a particular year, one-third of any increase in value is added in that year, and the balance added in equal increments over the following two years in the three-year cycle. For example, a property increasing in value from $72,000 to $84,000 would have a value for tax purposes of $76,000 the first year, $80,000 the second year and $84,000 the third year.

If, upon completion of the triennial review, the value of a property is found to have changed, the owner is sent a **notice of reassessment** that shows the property's assessment for the next three years; no other notice is sent until the new cycle begins three years later. Taxpayers who believe that their assessments are improper may appeal within 45 days of receiving notice of assessment.

PAYMENT

Since 1995, home buyers who occupy a property may elect either **annual or semiannual tax payments**. When this is done upon transfer of ownership, the requested mode of payment will affect collections for the following tax year.

In addition, future tax bills on all owner-occupied residential property will offer both one-payment and two-payment plans. Such owners will be offered this choice each year. Due dates for semiannual payment will be July 1—payable without interest by September 30—and January 1—payable without interest by January 31 of each tax year. Owners choosing semiannual payments will pay a service charge with the second installment as well as a reasonable amount for interest lost to the taxing authority while waiting for the second payment. If taxes are paid from a lender's escrow account, the tax is paid in annual or semiannual installments as directed by the property owner or borrower.

Counties were required, at the time of setting up this semiannual system, also to prepare their data processing systems for quarterly payments, which may be authorized by future legislation.

Lenders who accept responsibility to pay property taxes on the mortgaged properties collect the required funds in expense (escrow) accounts. They are required to pay those taxes within 45 days after the earlier of the following: (1) the first due date after their receipt of the tax bill or, (2) after funds collected by the lender are sufficient to pay the amount of taxes and interest due. Lenders who fail to pay taxes as provided above must bear any additional costs of penalties and interest.

PROPERTY TAX RELIEF

The **Homestead Tax Credit** is designed to protect owner-occupied residence assessments from the effects of rapid inflation. It automatically provides a credit against the real estate tax if the assessment on a dwelling increases by more than a percentage over the previous year as determined by the state legislature. The credit equals the amount by which the reassessment exceeds the established percentage and applies if certain conditions were met during the previous calendar year.

Since the Homestead Tax Credit does not take into account homeowners' ability to pay, the state legislature devised what is popularly known as the **circuit breaker**. After taking into account homeowners' net worth, gross annual income and assessed value of their property, this program, for homeowners of all ages, sets limits on the amount of residential property tax due. This relief must be applied for each year.

The owners of **unsold and unrented** single dwelling units or newly constructed or substantially rehabilitated commercial properties may be entitled to **tax credit**s not exceeding the property taxes on the improvements. The credit applies for no more than one year immediately following construction or substantial rehabilitation.

Special provision has also been made for **senior tenants,** age 60 or older, to receive as much as $600 from the State to offset property taxes. Asset and income limits are among certain restrictions that apply.

TRANSFER AND RECORDATION TAXES

Except as discussed in the following paragraph, in every written or oral agreement for the sale or other disposition of property, it is presumed, in the absence of any contrary provision in the agreement or the law, that the parties to the agreement intended that the cost of any recordation tax or any State or local transfer tax be shared equally between the grantor and grantee. This presumption does not apply to mortgages or deeds of trust.

The First-Time Maryland Home Buyer Closing Cost Reduction Act of 1995

This law provides that first-time home buyers will not pay the State transfer tax. In a transfer involving such a buyer, the State transfer tax of .5 percent is reduced to .25 percent, and must be paid by the seller. Furthermore, unless the parties in such a transaction agree to the contrary, the recordation taxes and local transfer taxes are to be paid by the seller. *First-time home buyers* are defined in the law as purchasers who have never before owned and occupied a principal residence in this State, will occupy the property as their principal residence and/or meet certain other requirements.

Under the same law, purchasers of residential real property for owner occupancy, may, at the time of settlement, choose semiannual payments for the ensuing tax years. This is intended to reduce the amount of *ad valorem* tax to be collected at settlement for escrow accounts.

CORPORATE FRANCHISE TAX

Most corporations are taxed annually on their franchise or right to do business in the State. The annual tax of $40 becomes a general lien on the property or the corporation and can be enforced against it. When a broker files for a real estate license and the brokerage is a corporation, the Commission requires that a copy of the brokerage's Articles of Incorporation be filed also.

PROPERTY TAX ASSESSMENT, AGRICULTURAL USE

Lands that are actively devoted to farm or agricultural use are assessed on the basis of such use and are not assessed as if subdivided. The State Department of Assessments and Taxation establishes criteria for the purpose of determining whether land qualifies for assessment as agricultural use. The State's purpose is to slow the conversion of farm lands to nonfarm uses.

The Agricultural Transfer Tax is calculated by the Assessments Office and is payable at the time the property transfer takes place. Details are discussed in Chapter 12 of this volume.

DELINQUENCY AND REDEMPTION

Taxes are due July 1 each year. Taxes that are not paid by September 30, or by January 31 if the two payment plan is used, are considered delinquent, bear interest as provided by law and are subject to a real estate tax sale held by the county treasurer. The dates and rules regarding such sales are made by each county. Tax-delinquent properties sold at a tax sale are not conveyed immediately to the buyer. There is a six-month statutory period of redemption during which the delinquent taxpayer may redeem the property by paying the county treasurer the amount of the delinquent tax plus the accumulated interest in penalty and related legal fees. The rate of redemption is established by law by various jurisdictions.

If no redemption is made during the six-month period, the tax sale buyer may apply to the court for the issuance of a deed to the property. Unpaid taxes create a priority lien on real property.

A number of tax program pamphlets are available in each county Tax Assessment Office.

LIENS

Mechanics' liens, as discussed in the text, are provided by state law to protect the rights of contractors, suppliers and other persons engaged to improve real estate. After the completion of work, contractors or suppliers have six months in which to record a notice of their lien. They then have one year from the date of recording to petition the courts to enforce the lien in the event the petition was not included when the lien was recorded.

Unperformed contracts (executory contracts) between contractors and subcontractors relating to construction, alteration or repair of a building, structure or improvement may not contain a provision that waives or requires the subcontractor to waive the right to claim a mechanic's lien or sue on a contractor's bond.

Buyers purchasing properties that have been recently improved or constructed should seek protection against possible outstanding mechanics' liens. In the usual purchase of real estate, the attorney for the buyer typically will have the responsibility to ascertain that the property being purchased is free from unpaid taxes and mechanics' or other outstanding liens. Special requirements regarding mechanics' liens for new home construction are noted in Chapter 11 of this volume.

RELEASE OF LIEN

When a lien on real property is satisfied, lienholders are required to mail or deliver a release of the lien within seven days after receiving payment. The release may be in the form of the original note, marked "paid" or "canceled." If lienholders fail to provide such a release after demand by the payor, the payor may bring action in the circuit court of the county where the property is located. In such an action, the lienholders or their agent may be liable for delivery of the release, as well as all costs and expenses of the action.

QUESTIONS

1. In Maryland, real estate taxes are imposed by

   a. cities and counties.
   b. special taxing districts.
   c. the state.
   d. All the above

2. All real property in Maryland is

   a. reassessed for tax purposes each year.
   b. assessed for tax purposes at the property's full market value.
   c. reassessed for tax purposes every three years.
   d. reassessed at time of resale.

3. Peter and Jayne Pauley own a contracting firm in Maryland. On February 1, 1999, Arch Campbell hired the Pauley firm to construct an addition to his five-bedroom house. The Pauleys finished work on the project on March 15; it is now April 15, and the Pauleys have not yet been paid. Based on this situation, which of the following is correct? The Pauleys have until

   a. August 1 to record a notice of lien.
   b. August 1 to enforce their mechanic's lien.
   c. September 15 to record a mechanic's lien.
   d. October 15 to enforce a mechanic's lien.

4. Ollie Akers has chosen to make semi-annual real estate tax payments on the home he occupies. Which of the following statements is false?

   a. Ollie's payments will be due July 1 and January 1 of each tax year.
   b. Ollie's first semiannual payment would be late if paid after September 30.
   c. Ollie's second semiannual payment would be late if paid after January 31.
   d. Ollie's second semiannual payment would be late if paid after March 31.

5. Ted Bolton has never before owned a principal residence in Maryland. He will settle on the purchase of a $100,000 home to occupy here in April. How will the State transfer tax be apportioned at settlement?

   a. Bolton will pay $0 and sellers will pay $500.
   b. Bolton will pay $250 and sellers will pay $250.
   c. Bolton will pay $0 and sellers will pay $250.
   d. The apportionment will be whatever Bolton and the sellers agree in the contract of sale.

11

Real Estate Contracts

OVERVIEW

In Maryland real estate contracts are used, among other things, for sales, rentals, options, and installment sales. A statewide sales agreement form, drafted in 1997 for the Maryland Association of REALTORS® (MAR), is in general use. Please see Figure 11.1. Students are strongly advised to obtain the updated version of this contract and its addenda when they become available after publication of this volume. The revised documents will reflect current law and practice concerning agency duties.

CAPACITY TO CONTRACT

Under Maryland law, a person reaches majority and has the capacity to enter into a valid real estate contract at age 18. However, minors married to persons who have reached the age of majority may enter into valid real estate contracts jointly with their spouses.

STATUTE OF FRAUDS

To be legally enforceable all contracts for the sale of real estate must be in writing and signed by the parties. Any oral (**parol**) transfer of an interest in real property for more than one year conveys no more than a tenancy at will. Other Maryland statutes require a 30-day notice to vacate under a tenancy at will.

The Maryland Statute of Frauds does not require a lease for a term of one year or less to be in writing to be enforceable. Regardless of this, all licensees are bound by regulation to reduce to signed, written form all agreements that they help negotiate.

STATUTE OF LIMITATIONS

Typically, suits to enforce a contract must be filed within three years of a breach of that contract. Specialty contracts have a 12-year statute of limitations.

CONTRACTS FOR THE SALE OF REAL ESTATE

Real estate sales and other contract forms should be drafted by attorneys. Licensees are authorized only to insert required information into such forms. Licensees who draft their own clauses or phrases could be accused of the misdemeanor "unauthorized practice of law."

Although licensees, unless otherwise qualified, cannot act as attorneys in their brokerage activities, they should nevertheless be sure that buyers and sellers understand that an executed sales contract is legally binding. Buyers and sellers should obtain legal counsel to interpret and approve the provisions of contracts.

To reduce confusion arising from the use of a wide variety of contract forms, the Maryland Association of REALTORS®, (MAR) working with its member associations and boards throughout the State, prepares a contract form designed to be used by its member brokers in residential sale transactions statewide. The MAR also provides contract language for 20 or more addenda. All these forms are copyrighted by the MAR and may not be altered or modified without the prior written express consent of the Association. MAR member-brokers are free to use the statewide forms or to have counsel draft forms for their firms' use.

Information That Must Be Included In Contracts

In certain circumstances, Maryland statutes require that licensees include specific information in contracts. Unless otherwise specifically agreed, a contract of sale is generally **not** made invalid by omission of required clauses such as those discussed below.

Contracts for the sale of improved residential real property must disclose the **estimated cost of any deferred water and sewer charges** for which the purchaser may become liable. Violation of this disclosure requirement entitles the initial purchaser to recover from the seller two times the amount of deferred charges the purchaser would be obligated to pay during the five years of payments following the sale.

Licensees acting as sellers or purchasers of real estate must notify the other party of that fact. This notification must be in writing, typically within the contract itself.

A real estate sales contract must indicate whether there is a **ground rent or leasehold interest** involved in the sale. If the ground rent is irredeemable, this fact must be indicated. If the ground rent is to be redeemed at the time of settlement, responsibility for notice, costs of redemption, etc., should be fixed as part of the written agreement. A contract for the sale of real property subject to a ground rent must contain a notice of the existence of the ground rent and notice that if ground rent is not timely paid the reversionary owner of the ground rent may bring an action for possession against the ground rent tenant and as a result of the action may own the property in fee.

The Brokers Act requires that every contract for use in the sale of residential property used as a dwelling place for one or two single-family units must contain the following statement in conspicuous type or handwritten:

Section 14-104 of the *Real Property Article* of the Annotated Code of Maryland provides that, unless otherwise negotiated in the contract or provided by local law, the cost of any recordation tax or any state or local transfer tax shall be shared equally between the buyer and seller.

Notwithstanding the statement above, the First-Time Home Buyers Closing Cost Reduction Act of 1995 reduces the State transfer tax in the case of first-time home buyers, from .5 percent to .25 percent. That entire amount must be paid by the seller. In such a transaction, the seller must also pay the entire amount of recordation and local transfer tax, unless there is an express agreement between the parties to the contrary. Other details of this issue appear in Chapter 10 of this volume.

If the property is subject to a **homeowners association (HOA)**, and to the imposition of mandatory HOA fees, this must be disclosed to purchasers, preferably by reference within the purchase agreement.

Contracts for the sale of real estate must contain a notice of purchaser's protection by the **Real Estate Guaranty Fund** in an amount not to exceed $25,000.

A real estate broker must **deposit all earnest (deposit) monies** in a special non-interest-bearing account unless directed to do otherwise by both buyer and seller.

The Brokers Act mandates that contracts reveal that buyers of single-family dwellings may not be required to employ specific title insurance, settlement or escrow companies or title attorneys, but may choose their own. (See Part I of this volume.)

The seller is required to notify the purchaser that the land being transferred may be subject to **agricultural land transfer tax**. Sellers who fail to notify buyers as required are liable to the buyers for the agricultural land transfer tax which the buyer will have to pay.

Other Required Clauses

The *Real Property Article* requires that contracts of sale must also include the following notices and disclosures, where applicable:

- Notice pertaining to sale of real property in Prince George's County creating subdivision
- Notice pertaining to resale of condominium unit
- Notice pertaining to initial sale of lot in development containing more than 12 lots
- Notice pertaining to resale of any lot or initial sale of lot in development containing 12 or fewer lots
- Notice pertaining to initial sale of lot not intended to be occupied or rented for residential purposes
- Notice pertaining to initial sale of cooperative interests
- Notice of liability for agricultural land transfer tax
- Notice to purchaser pertaining to sale of certain land in Prince George's County, that the land being sold is subject to a development impact fee, and the unpaid amount of that fee
- Notice pertaining to sale of certain agriculturally assessed land in St. Mary's and Charles Counties

Baltimore City and most counties have various additional contract requirements unique to their jurisdictions. Information about these requirements is available from local boards or associations for use by their members. For example, contracts for the sale of multiple-dwelling property in Baltimore City must contain a clause whereby the seller guarantees that the property being purchased complies with the Baltimore City Multiple-Dwelling Code and that the license will be delivered to the buyer at the time of settlement.

Property in Maryland not served by public sewer and water is subject to the State Department of Health and Mental Hygiene laws and regulations pertaining to individual sewage disposal systems and wells. The licensee must provide the buyer of unimproved land with a notice that if the property being purchased is to be used for residential purposes the buyer, before signing the contract, should ascertain the status of sewerage and water facilities and, if required, whether the property will be approved for installation of a well and/or private sewerage system.

The Department of Veterans Affairs (DVA), the Federal Housing Administration (FHA) and many private lenders require an evaluation by the local health department of the sewage disposal system and the water supply on residential property prior to settlement. When this is required, a bacteriological sample must be collected from the well and analyzed by the health department. Consequently, licensees involved in such a transaction must allow sufficient time for these procedures when estimating a settlement date. Assistance and information are available from the Department of Health and Mental Hygiene, O'Conor Building, 201 West Preston Street, Baltimore, MD 21201, or from local health boards.

Contingency and Other Clauses

To express the exact agreements of the parties to a contract and to protect the best interests of their clients, licensees often employ contingency clauses. They should avoid drafting the language of such clauses and make use of clauses with wording drafted by competent legal counsel. These are often available, along with basic contract forms, in collections of standard contract addenda available to brokers through their real estate boards and associations.

Release from Contract of Sale

When one party is unable or unwilling to consummate a contract of sale and the other party agrees to release that party, the broker should provide a competently drafted release form for their signatures. This release should also direct the broker how to dispose of any earnest money deposit. If the parties cannot agree how to dispose of the deposit, the broker must follow statutory procedures outlined in Part I of this volume for such a situation.

OPTION AGREEMENTS

In Maryland, a **lease option agreement** is defined as any lease agreement containing a clause that gives the tenant some power to purchase the landlord's interest in real property. No lease option purchase of improved residential property is valid in Maryland unless it contains the statement in capital letters "THIS IS NOT A CONTRACT TO BUY" and a clear statement of the option agreement's purpose and effect with respect to the purchase of the property that is the subject of the option. Even though details of times, prices, dates, etc.—everything needed for a contract of sale—may be clearly set forth, the option ". . . IS NOT A CONTRACT TO BUY."

CONSTRUCTION CONTRACTS

Prior to the signing of a contract for the construction of a single-family dwelling using alternating current (AC) electrical service and a public water system, a builder must, under certain conditions, offer to a prospective buyer the option of having the builder install a sprinkler system.

NEW HOME WARRANTIES

Before entering into contracts for sale or construction of new homes, builders must disclose to purchasers on a State-mandated form whether they participate in a new home warranty security plan and the extent of that plan.

If builders do not participate in a new home warranty plan, they must disclose, among other things, that without a new home warranty the purchaser may be afforded only certain limited warranties. The disclosure must also state that builders of new homes are not required to be licensed by the state and are not licensed in most local jurisdictions. Purchasers who

acknowledge by their signature that they have been so informed have five working days to rescind their contract and recover all money paid for their purchases. Contracts for purchase or construction of new homes that do not contain this notice are voidable by the buyers.

Any person knowingly misrepresenting the existence of a new home warranty is subject to a fine not exceeding $50,000 or imprisonment for not more than two years or both, in addition to other penalties provided by the *Real Property Article*.

INSTALLMENT CONTRACTS

Maryland statutes provide protections for purchasers of residential property under installment contracts, which are stronger than provided by common law. Maryland requirements concerning installment contracts for the sale of real estate are presented in Chapter 14/15 of this volume. The main text covers general information on installment contracts.

ESCROW AGREEMENTS

The escrow procedure of closing a real estate transaction, as described in the main text, is rarely used in Maryland. Settlement meetings with absolute delivery of the title to purchasers are much more common. Closing is discussed in Chapter 22 of this volume.

DISCLOSURE REQUIREMENTS ON CONDOMINIUM SALES

A contract for the initial sale or resale of a condominium unit requires the disclosure of certain information to the purchaser before the execution of the contract. The buyer of a condominium unit has 15 days (for initial sale) or seven days (for resale) within which the contract may be rescinded. A contract for the initial sale of a residential condominium unit to a member of the public must contain a notice of the developer's warranties.

RECEIPT OF EARNEST MONEY

All earnest money deposits received by brokers in connection with an offer to purchase, as well as any other deposits of money belonging to other parties, must be promptly deposited and retained by brokers in a bank account separate from their own in an institution in Maryland approved by a federal or state agency. Buyers may instruct a broker not to deposit their earnest money until such time as their offer to purchase has been accepted by the seller. Such instructions would typically be included in their sales contract.

DEPOSITS ON NEW HOMES

In connection with the sale and purchase of new single-family residential units, including condominiums that are not completed at the time of contracting the sale, if the vendor or builder obligates purchasers to pay any sum of money before units have been completed and the realty granted to the purchaser, the builder or vendor is required to

- deposit or hold the sums in an escrow account to ensure their return to purchasers who are entitled to them or

- obtain and maintain a corporate surety bond to provide return of deposits to purchasers who are entitled to them.

The Maryland Custom Home Protection Act, found in the *Real Property Article*, provides protection for buyers of newly constructed homes. This law sets standards for contract payments, surety bonds, contract requirements, mortgage loans, and sales by licensed real estate brokers. Detailed provisions govern brokers' handling of deposit monies.

RESIDENTIAL PROPERTY DISCLOSURE AND DISCLAIMER STATEMENT

The required use of the Property Disclosure and Disclaimer Statement is presented in Chapter 6 of this volume at **Property Disclosure Requirements**. Be sure to review it. The Disclosure and Disclaimer Statement need **not** be used in

- the initial sale of a single-family residential real property that has never been occupied or for which a certificate of occupancy has been issued within 1 year before the seller and buyer enter into a contract of sale;
- the transfer of properties exempt from transfer tax under the *Tax-Property Article* (land installment contracts and certain options to purchase do require the use of the statement);
- sale by a lender, or affiliate or subsidiary of a lender, of property acquired by foreclosure or deed in lieu of foreclosure;

- a sheriff's sale, tax sale or sale by foreclosure, partition or by court appointed trustee;
- a transfer by a fiduciary in the course of the administration of a decedent's estate, guardianship, conservatorship or trust;
- the transfer of a single-family residential real property to be converted by the buyer into use other than residential use or to be demolished; or
- the sale of unimproved real property.

POWER OF ATTORNEY

An attorney-in-fact can execute a Maryland real estate transaction. When a deed, mortgage or other instrument is signed under a power of attorney, the power of attorney document itself—properly signed and acknowledged—must be recorded before the deed or mortgage can be placed in the public record. It is prudent to check with settlement officers before closing to make sure such powers of attorney are in a form acceptable to them.

DUTIES AND OBLIGATIONS OF LICENSEES

The Regulations of the Commission set forth a number of duties and obligations that the real estate licensee has toward clients, the public and fellow licensees with respect to contracts. Many of these duties apply to contracts. They include prompt presentation of all written offers and counteroffers, reduction of all agreements to a written form that sets forth all the obligations of the parties, seeking proper signatures on all forms and giving and retaining of copies of all signed agreements.

EQUITABLE TITLE

When a contract of sale is signed by all parties, the buyers are considered to receive **equitable title**. Maryland has not set aside the common law principle that equitable title places the risk of loss due to accidental damage to the premises on the buyers until they occupy the property. Most contracts, therefore, include a provision that the sellers will maintain—until settlement or occupancy, whichever occurs first—full insurance on the property and bear the risk of loss due to damage of the property. Licensees should see that this issue is addressed in any contract they negotiate.

RESIDENTIAL SALES CONTRACT PROVIDED STATEWIDE FOR MARYLAND REALTORS®

The residential sales contract form which appears as Figure 11.1 on following five pages, is provided to members of the Maryland Association of REALTORS® for their exclusive use. The Association also provides a wide variety of addenda for specific situations and to meet certain legal requirements. Examples are the Lead-Based Paint Hazard Inspection Addendum, required by Federal law in residential sales of structures built before 1978, and the First-Time Maryland Home Buyer Transfer and Recordation Tax Addendum.

Figure 11.1   Maryland Association of REALTORS® Residential Sales Contract (Page 1 of 5)

RESIDENTIAL CONTRACT OF SALE

This is a Legally Binding Contract; If Not Understood, Seek Competent Legal Advice.

THIS FORM IS DESIGNED AND INTENDED FOR THE SALE AND PURCHASE OF IMPROVED SINGLE FAMILY RESIDENTIAL REAL ESTATE LOCATED IN MARYLAND ONLY. *FOR OTHER TYPES OF PROPERTY INCLUDE APPROPRIATE ADDENDA.*

BROKER: _____   BRANCH OFFICE: _____

OFFICE PHONE NO: _____   FAX NO: _____   BROKER/AGENT ID NO: _____

SALES ASSOCIATE: _____   PHONE NO: _____

ACTING AS   ☐ SELLER AGENT (WHETHER "COOPERATING AGENT" OR "SELLING AGENT"); OR
            ☐ BUYER AGENT; OR
            ☐ DISCLOSED DUAL AGENT OF SELLER AND BUYER

IN COOPERATION WITH

BROKER: _____   BRANCH OFFICE: _____

OFFICE PHONE NO: _____   FAX NO: _____   BROKER/AGENT ID NO: _____

SALES ASSOCIATE: _____   PHONE NO: _____

ACTING AS   ☐ LISTING BROKER AND SELLER AGENT; OR
            ☐ DISCLOSED DUAL AGENT OF SELLER AND BUYER

TIME IS OF THE ESSENCE UNLESS BOTH BUYER AND SELLER INITIAL HERE _____ _____ _____ _____

1. DATE OF OFFER: _____ , 19_____

2. SELLER: NAME: _____

   CURRENT ADDRESS: _____ ZIP: _____

   AND

3. BUYER: NAME: _____

   CURRENT ADDRESS: _____ ZIP: _____

4. PROPERTY DESCRIPTION: Seller does sell to Buyer and Buyer does purchase from Seller, all of the following described Property

(hereinafter "Property") known as _____

located in _____ City/County, Maryland, Zip _____ together with the improvements thereon, and all rights and appurtenances thereto belonging.

5. ESTATE: The Property is being conveyed: _____ in fee simple or _____ subject to an annual ground rent, now existing or to be created, in the

amount of _____ Dollars ($_____) payable semi-annually, as now or to be recorded among

the Land Records of _____ City/County, Maryland. If the Property is subject to ground rent and the ground rent is not timely paid, the owner of the reversionary interest (i.e., the person to whom the ground rent is payable) may bring an action of ejectment against the leasehold owner pursuant to Section 8-402.2 of the Real Property Article, Annotated Code of Maryland (as amended). As a result of this action, the owner of the reversionary interest may obtain title to the Property in fee, discharged from the lease.

6. PURCHASE PRICE: The purchase price is _____

Dollars ($_____).

7. SETTLEMENT: Settlement shall be on _____ 19 _____ or sooner if agreed to in writing by both parties.

The parties acknowledge pages 1 through 5 of this contract of sale.	BUYER	BUYER	SELLER	SELLER

Page 1 of 5 - Revision #3 - 9/97

Source: This form has been made available through the courtesy of the Maryland Association of REALTORS® and is protected by the copyright laws.

Figure 11.1   Maryland Association of REALTORS® Residential Sales Contract (Page 2 of 5)

8. SETTLEMENT COSTS: NOTICE TO BUYER, BUYER HAS THE RIGHT TO SELECT BUYER'S OWN TITLE INSURANCE COMPANY, TITLE LAWYER, SETTLEMENT COMPANY, ESCROW COMPANY, MORTGAGE LENDER, OR FINANCIAL INSTITUTION AS DEFINED IN THE FINANCIAL INSTITUTIONS ARTICLE, ANNOTATED CODE OF MARYLAND. BUYER ACKNOWLEDGES THAT SELLER MAY NOT BE PROHIBITED FROM OFFERING OWNER FINANCING AS A CONDITION OF SETTLEMENT. Buyer agrees to pay all other settlement costs and charges including, but not limited to, all Lender's fees in connection herewith, including title examination and title insurance fees, all document preparation and recording fees, notary fees, survey fees where required, and all recording charges, except those incident to clearing existing encumbrances or title defects, except if Buyer is a Veteran obtaining VA financing, those prohibited to be paid by a Veteran obtaining VA financing or except if Buyer is obtaining FHA financing, those prohibited to be paid by a Buyer obtaining FHA financing, which prohibited charges shall be paid by Seller.

9. TRANSFER CHARGES: SECTION 14-104 OF THE REAL PROPERTY ARTICLE OF THE ANNOTATED CODE OF MARYLAND PROVIDES THAT, UNLESS OTHERWISE NEGOTIATED IN THE CONTRACT OR PROVIDED BY STATE OR LOCAL LAW, THE COST OF ANY RECORDATION TAX OR ANY STATE OR LOCAL TRANSFER TAX SHALL BE SHARED EQUALLY BETWEEN THE BUYER AND SELLER. Unless otherwise provided by an addendum to this Contract, the costs of state and local transfer and recordation taxes (other than agricultural land transfer tax) shall be shared equally by Buyer and Seller. (If First-Time Maryland Home Buyer: See Transfer and Recordation Tax Addendum.)

10. ADJUSTMENTS: Ground rent, homeowner's association fees, rent and water rent shall be adjusted and apportioned as of date of settlement, and all taxes, general or special, and all other public or governmental charges or assessments against the Property which are or may be payable on a periodic basis, including Metropolitan District Sanitary Commission or other benefit charges, assessments, liens or encumbrances for sewer, water, drainage, paving, or other public improvements completed or commenced on or prior to the date hereof, or subsequent thereto, are to be adjusted and apportioned as of the date of settlement and are to be assumed and paid thereafter by Buyer, whether assessments have been levied or not as of date of settlement if applicable by local law. Any heating or cooking fuels remaining in supply tank(s) at time of settlement shall become the property of the Buyer.

11. TERMITE INSPECTION: Buyer, at Buyer's expense is authorized to obtain a written report from a Maryland licensed pest control company that, based on a careful visual inspection, there is no evidence of termite or other wood-destroying insect infestation in the residence, including garage, but not including fences or other outbuildings (unless within 3 feet of main dwelling and/or garage) and, if such infestation previously existed, it has been corrected, and any damage due to such infestation has been corrected. The provisions of this paragraph shall apply to the entirety of any outbuilding(s) located within three feet of the main dwelling and/or garage and shall apply to ten (10) linear feet of the nearest portion of any fence within three feet of the main dwelling and/or garage. If any such infestation is present, or if any evidence of damage caused by such present or prior infestation is discovered, Seller, at Seller's expense, shall treat such infestation and repair any damage caused by such present or prior infestation. However, if the cost of treatment and repair of such damage exceeds 2% of the purchase price, Seller may, at Seller's option, cancel this Contract, unless the Buyer, at the Buyer's option, should choose to pay for the cost of treatment and repairs exceeding 2% of the purchase price, then this Contract shall remain in full force and effect. If such report reveals damage for which the cost of treatment and repair may exceed 2% of the purchase price, Seller's decision regarding treatment and repair of damage shall be communicated in writing to Buyer within five (5) days from receipt of the report, after which Buyer shall respond to Seller in writing with Buyer's decision within three (3) days from receipt of Seller's notification of Seller's decision. If Seller does not notify Buyer in writing of Seller's decision within five (5) days from receipt of report, Buyer may, at Buyer's option, pay for the cost of treatment and repairs exceeding 2% of the purchase price. If Buyer does not want to pay for the cost of treatment and repairs exceeding 2% of the purchase price, Buyer may terminate this Contract upon written notice delivered to Seller. In the event this Contract is terminated under the terms of this paragraph, then all monies on deposit shall be returned to Buyer in accordance with the terms of this Contract.

12. CONDITION OF PROPERTY AND POSSESSION: At settlement, Seller shall deliver possession of the Property and shall deliver the Property vacant, clear of trash and debris, broom clean and in substantially the same condition as existed on the date of Contract acceptance. All electrical, heating, air conditioning (if any), plumbing (including well and septic), and any other mechanical systems and related equipment, appliances and smoke detector(s) included in this Contract will be in working condition. Buyer reserves the right to inspect the Property within five (5) days prior to settlement. **EXCEPT AS OTHERWISE SPECIFIED IN THIS CONTRACT, THE PROPERTY IS SOLD "AS IS".**

13. SALE/SETTLEMENT OR LEASE OF OTHER REAL ESTATE: Neither this Contract nor the granting of Buyer's loan referred to herein is to be conditioned or contingent in any manner upon the sale, settlement and/or lease of any other real estate unless a contingency for the sale, settlement and/or lease of other real estate is contained in an addendum to this Contract. Unless this Contract is expressly contingent upon the sale, settlement and/or lease of any other real estate, Buyer shall not apply for or accept a financing loan commitment which is contingent upon or requires as a precondition to funding that any other real estate be sold, settled and/or leased.

14. BUYER RESPONSIBILITY: If Buyer has misrepresented Buyer's financial ability to consummate the purchase of the Property, or if this Contract is contingent upon Buyer securing a written commitment for financing and Buyer fails to apply for such financing within the time period herein specified, or fails to pursue financing diligently and in good faith, or if Buyer makes any misrepresentations in any document relating to financing, or takes (or fails to take) any action which causes Buyer's disqualification for financing, then Buyer shall be in default and Seller may elect by written notice to Buyer, to terminate this Contract and/or pursue the remedies set forth under the **"Default"** Paragraph 16.

15. SELLER RESPONSIBILITY: Seller agrees to keep existing mortgages free of default until settlement. All violation notices or requirements noted or issued by any governmental authority, or actions in any court on account thereof, against or affecting the Property at the date of settlement of this Contract, shall be complied with by the Seller and the Property conveyed free thereof.

16. DEFAULT: Buyer and Seller are required and agree to make full settlement in accordance with the terms of this Contract and acknowledge that failure to do so constitutes a breach hereof. If Buyer fails to make full settlement or is in default due to Buyer's failure to comply with the terms, covenants and conditions of this Contract, the deposit can be retained by Seller as long as a release of deposit agreement is signed and executed by all parties, expressing that said deposit can be retained by Seller. In the event that the parties do not agree to execute a release of deposit, Buyer and Seller shall have all legal and equitable remedies. If Seller fails to make full settlement or is in default due to Seller's failure to comply with the terms, covenants and conditions of this Contract, Buyer shall be entitled to pursue such rights and remedies as may be available, at law or in equity, including, without limitation, an action for specific performance of this Contract and/or monetary damages. In the event of any litigation or dispute between Seller and Buyer concerning the release of the deposit, Broker's sole responsibility may be met, at Broker's option, by paying the deposit into the court in which such litigation is pending, or by paying the deposit into the court of proper jurisdiction by an action of interpleader. Buyer and Seller agree that, upon Broker's payment of the deposit into court, neither Buyer nor Seller shall have any further right, claim, demand or action against Broker regarding the release of the deposit and Buyer and Seller, jointly and severally, shall indemnify and hold the Broker harmless from any and all such rights, claims, demands or actions. In the event of such dispute and election by the Broker to file an action of interpleader as herein provided, Buyer and Seller further agree and hereby expressly and irrevocably authorize the Broker to deduct from the deposit all costs incurred by the Broker in the filing and maintenance of such action of interpleader including but not limited to filing fees, court costs, service of process fees and attorneys' fees, provided that the amount deducted shall not exceed the lesser of $500 or the amount of the deposit held by the Broker. All such fees and costs authorized herein to be deducted may be deducted by Broker from the deposit prior to paying the balance of the deposit to the court. Buyer and Seller further agree and expressly declare that all such fees and costs so deducted shall be the exclusive property of the Broker. If the amount deducted by the Broker is less than the total of all of the costs incurred by the Broker in filing and maintaining the interpleader action, then Seller and Buyer jointly, and severally, agree to reimburse the Broker for all such excess costs upon the conclusion of the interpleader action.

Figure 11.1   Maryland Association of REALTORS® Residential Sales Contract (Page 3 of 5)

17. PAYMENT TERMS: The payment of the purchase price shall be made by Buyer as follows:
(a) An initial deposit by way of _____ , in the amount of _____ Dollars ($ _____) at the time of this offer. (b) An additional deposit by way of _____ , in the amount of _____ Dollars ($_____) to be paid within _____ (_____) days from the date of Contract acceptance. (c) The purchase price less any and all deposits shall be paid in full by Buyer in cash, wired funds, bank check or by certified check at settlement. _____
(d) All deposits will be held in escrow by: _____

18. FINANCING: This Contract is contingent upon buyer obtaining a written commitment for a loan secured by the Property as follows:

CHECK ☐ No Financing Contingency   ☐ Gift of Funds Addendum
       ☐ Attached FHA Financing Addendum   ☐ Conventional Loan as follows:
       ☐ Attached VA Financing Addendum   Loan Amount $ _____
       ☐ Attached Assumption Addendum   Term of Note _____ Years
       ☐ Attached Owner Financing Addendum   Amortization _____ Years
       ☐ Conventional Loan Assumption Addendum   Interest Rate _____ %
       ☐ Wrap Around Mortgage Addendum   Loan Program _____

19. FINANCING APPLICATION AND COMMITMENT: Buyer agrees to make written application for the financing as herein described within _____ (____) days from the date of Contract acceptance. If such written financing commitment is not obtained by Buyer within _____ (____) days from the date of Contract acceptance, this Contract of Sale shall be null and void and of no further legal effect, and all deposits hereunder shall be disbursed in accordance with the terms of this Contract. If Buyer has complied with all of Buyer's obligations under this Contract, including those with respect to applying for financing and seeking to obtain financing, then the release of deposit agreement shall provide that all monies on deposit shall be returned to Buyer.

20. ALTERNATE FINANCING: Buyer may obtain a written commitment for financing in which the interest, terms of payment, amount of loan, or any one of these differs from the financing conditions herein set forth, and, if so, the preceding financing conditions of the Contract shall be deemed to have been fully satisfied. This alternate financing may not increase costs to Seller or exceed the time allowed to secure the financing commitment as stated herein. Nothing in this paragraph shall relieve Buyer of the obligation to apply for and diligently pursue the financing described in the "Financing" Paragraph #19.

21. DEPOSIT: Buyer hereby authorizes and directs the Broker as specified in Paragraph 17-d of this Contract to hold the initial deposit instrument without negotiation or deposit until the parties have executed and accepted this Contract. Upon acceptance, the initial deposit shall be expeditiously placed in escrow as provided below. If Seller does not execute and accept this Contract, the initial deposit instrument shall be promptly returned to the Buyer. Brokers may charge a fee for establishing an interest bearing account. Seller and Buyer instruct the Broker to place all deposit monies in:
   ☐ A non-interest bearing account.
   ☐ An interest bearing account, the interest on which, in absence of default by the Buyer, shall accrue to the benefit of the Buyer.
The deposit shall be disbursed by the Broker at settlement. In the event this Contract shall be terminated or settlement does not occur, Buyer and Seller agree that the deposit shall be disbursed by Broker only in accordance with a release of deposit agreement executed by Buyer and Seller.

22. CONVENTIONAL LOAN LENDER FEE/CHARGES: Buyer agrees to pay to the Lender loan origination/loan discount fees of ____ % of the Loan Amount and Seller agrees to pay loan origination/loan discount fees of ____ % of the Loan Amount. Buyer shall receive the benefit of any reduction in said fees. All loan insurance premiums as required by Lender shall be paid by Buyer. If the existing loan is to be transferred to/assumed by Buyer, Buyer agrees to pay all fees and charges required by Lender.

23. INCLUSIONS/EXCLUSIONS: Included in the purchase price are all permanently attached fixtures, including all smoke detectors. Certain other **now existing items** which may be considered personal property, whether installed or stored upon the property, are included or excluded, as follows (if neither column is checked, item shall be considered excluded):

INCLUDED YES NO	INCLUDED YES NO	INCLUDED YES NO	INCLUDED YES NO
☐ ☐ Stove or Range	☐ ☐ Dishwasher	☐ ☐ Ceiling Fan(s) #	☐ ☐ Alarm System
☐ ☐ Cooktop	☐ ☐ Freezer	☐ ☐ Clothes Washer	☐ ☐ Intercom
☐ ☐ Wall Oven(s) #___	☐ ☐ Window Fan(s) # ___	☐ ☐ Clothes Dryer	☐ ☐ Storage Shed(s) #___
☐ ☐ Refrigerator(s) #___	☐ ☐ Fireplace Screen/Doors	☐ ☐ Furnace Humidifier	☐ ☐ Garage Opener(s) #___
☐ ☐ w/ice maker	☐ ☐ Pool, Equip. & Cover	☐ ☐ Electronic Air Filter	☐ ☐ w/remote(s)#___
☐ ☐ Built-in Microwave	☐ ☐ Hot Tub, Equip. & Cover	☐ ☐ Water Filter	☐ ☐ Playgrnd. Equipment
☐ ☐ Trash Compactor	☐ ☐ Screens	☐ ☐ Water Softener	☐ ☐ Wood Stove
☐ ☐ Exist. W/W Carpet	☐ ☐ Storm Windows	☐ ☐ Drapery/Curtains	☐ ☐ T.V. Antenna
☐ ☐ Disposal	☐ ☐ Storm Doors	☐ ☐ Drapery/Curtain Rods	☐ ☐ Satellite Dish
☐ ☐ Exhaust Fan(s)	☐ ☐ Window A/C Unit(s) # __	☐ ☐ Shades/Blinds	☐ ☐ Central Vacuum

ADDITIONAL INCLUSIONS (SPECIFY): _____

ADDITIONAL EXCLUSIONS (SPECIFY): _____

24. AGENCY CONFIRMATION: The Seller and the Buyer each confirm that disclosure of the agency relationships as described in this Contract conforms with the agency relationships previously agreed to in writing.

25. BROKER'S FEE: All parties irrevocably instruct the settlement agent to collect the fee or compensation and disburse same according to the terms and conditions provided in the listing agreement and/or agency representation agreement. Settlement shall not be a condition precedent to payment of compensation.

26. BROKER LIABILITY: Brokers, their agents, subagents and employees do not assume any responsibility for the condition of the Property or for the performance of this Contract by any or all parties hereto. By signing this Contract, Buyer and Seller acknowledge that they have not relied on any representations made by the Brokers, or any agents, subagents or employees of the Brokers, except those representations expressly set forth in this Contract.

27. MEDIATION: In the event a dispute between Buyer and Seller arises out of or from this Contract or the transaction which is the subject of this Contract, Buyer and Seller acknowledge that such dispute may be voluntarily submitted to mediation through the Local Board/Association of Realtors® (if available), the Maryland Association of REALTORS®,Inc. or through such other mediator or mediation service as mutually agreed upon by Buyer and Seller, in writing. Mediation is a process by which the parties attempt to resolve a dispute with the assistance of a neutral mediator who is trained to facilitate the resolution of disputes. The mediation process requires the voluntary participation by both Buyer and Seller. The mediator has no authority to make an award, to impose a resolution of the dispute upon the parties or to require the parties to continue mediation if either party does not desire to do so. A resolution of a dispute through mediation is not binding upon the parties unless the parties enter into a written agreement resolving the dispute.

Page 3 of 5 - Revision #3 - 9/97

Figure 11.1   Maryland Association of REALTORS® Residential Sales Contract (Page 4 of 5)

28. ATTORNEY'S FEES: In any action or proceeding involving a dispute between the Buyer and the Seller arising out of this Contract, the prevailing party shall be entitled to receive from the other party, reasonable attorney's fees as determined by the court or arbitrator. In the event of any dispute between Seller and Buyer or between Seller and Broker(s) and/or Buyer and Broker(s) resulting in Broker(s) or any agents, subagents or employees of Broker(s) being made a party to such dispute, including, but not limited to, any litigation, arbitration, or complaint and claim before the Maryland Real Estate Commission, whether as defendant, cross-defendant, third-party defendant or respondent, Seller and Buyer, jointly and severally, agree to indemnify and hold Broker(s) and any agents, subagents and employees of Brokers harmless from any liability, loss, cost, damage or expense (including filing fees, court costs, service of process fees, transcript fees and attorneys' fees), resulting therefrom, provided that such dispute does not result in a judgment against Broker(s), Broker(s)' agents, subagents or employees for acting improperly.

29. NON-ASSIGNABILITY: This Contract may not be assigned without the written consent of the Buyer and the Seller. If the Buyer and the Seller agree in writing to an assignment of this Contract, the original parties to this Contract remain obligated hereunder until settlement.

30. LEASES: Seller may not negotiate new leases or renew existing leases on the property which extend beyond settlement or possession date without Buyer's written consent.

31. PROPERTY INSURANCE AND RISK OF LOSS: The Property is to be held at the risk of Seller until legal title has passed or possession has been given to Buyer. If, prior to the time legal title has passed or possession has been given to Buyer, whichever shall occur first, all or a substantial part of the Property is destroyed or damaged, without fault of Buyer, then this Contract, at the option of Buyer, upon written notice to Seller, shall be null and void and of no further effect, and all deposits hereunder shall be returned to Buyer in accordance with the terms of this Contract.

32. NOTICE TO THE PARTIES: THE BROKERS, THEIR AGENTS, SUBAGENTS AND EMPLOYEES, MAKE NO REPRESENTATIONS WITH RESPECT TO THE FOLLOWING:

A. Water quality, color, or taste or operating conditions of private water systems.

B. Location, size or operating condition of private septic systems.

C. The extensions of public utilities by local municipal authorities, existence or availability of public utilities, and any assessments, fees or costs for public utilities which might be imposed by local municipal authorities, should public utilities be extended or available to the subject Property. (The Buyer should consult the Department of Public Works to determine the availability of proposed future extensions of utilities.)

D. Lot size and exact location. If the subject Property is part of a recorded subdivision, the Buyer can review the plat upon request at the Record Office. If the subject Property is not part of a recorded subdivision, the Buyer may verify exact size and location through a survey by a registered engineer or land surveyor, at Buyer's expense.

E. Existing zoning or permitted uses of the Property. Buyer should verify with the Zoning Office and/or a licensed engineer to determine zoning and permitted uses.

F. Brokers/agents are not advising the parties as to certain other issues, including without limitation: soil conditions; flood hazard areas; possible restrictions of the use of property due to restrictive covenants, subdivision, environmental laws, easements or other documents; airport or aircraft noise; planned land use, roads or highways; and construction materials and/or hazardous materials, including without limitation flame retardant treated plywood (FRT), radon, urea formaldehyde foam insulation (UFFI), asbestos, and lead based paint. Information relating to these issues may be available from appropriate governmental authorities. This disclosure is not intended to provide an inspection contingency.

33. *SINGLE FAMILY RESIDENTIAL REAL PROPERTY DISCLOSURE NOTICE: BUYER IS ADVISED OF THE RIGHT TO RECEIVE A DISCLOSURE AND DISCLAIMER STATEMENT FROM SELLER. (SECTION 10-702 REAL PROPERTY ARTICLE, ANNOTATED CODE OF MARYLAND.)*

34. DEED AND TITLE: Upon payment of the purchase price, a deed for the Property containing covenants of special warranty shall be executed by the Seller and shall convey the Property to Buyer. Title to the Property, including all chattels included in the purchase, shall be good and merchantable, free of liens and encumbrances except as specified herein; except for use and occupancy restrictions of public record which are generally applicable to properties in the immediate neighborhood or the subdivision in which the Property is located and publicly recorded easements for public utilities and any other easements which may be observed by an inspection of the Property. Buyer expressly assumes the risk that restrictive covenants, zoning laws or other recorded documents may restrict or prohibit the use of the Property for the purpose(s) intended by Buyer. In the event Seller is unable to give good and merchantable title or such as can be insured by a Maryland licensed title insurer, with Buyer paying not more than the standard rate as filed with the Maryland Insurance Commissioner, Seller, at Seller's expense, shall have the option of curing any defect so as to enable Seller to give good and merchantable title or, if Buyer is willing to accept title without said defect being cured, paying any special premium on behalf of Buyer to obtain title insurance on the Property to the benefit of Buyer. In the event Seller elects to cure any defects in title, this Contract shall continue to remain in full force and effect and the date of settlement shall be extended for a period not to exceed fourteen (14) additional days. If Seller is unable to cure such title defect(s) and is unable to obtain a policy of title insurance on the benefit of Buyer from a Maryland licensed title insurer, Buyer shall have the option of taking such title as Seller can give, or terminating this Contract and being reimbursed by the Seller for cost for searching title as may have been incurred not to exceed 1/2 of 1% of the purchase price. In the latter event, there shall be no further liability or obligation on either of the parties hereto and this Contract shall become null and void and all deposits hereunder shall be returned to Buyer in accordance with the terms of this Contract. In no event shall the Brokers or their agents have any liability for any defect in Seller's title.

35. WETLANDS NOTICE: The Buyer is advised that if all or a portion of the Property being purchased is wetlands, the approval of the U.S. Army Corps of Engineers will be necessary before a building permit can be issued for the Property. Additionally, the future use of existing dwellings may be restricted due to wetlands. The Corps has adopted a broad definition of wetlands which encompasses a large portion of the Chesapeake Bay Region. Other portions of the State may also be considered wetlands. For information as to whether the Property includes wetlands, you may contact the Baltimore District of the U.S. Army Corps of Engineers. You may also elect, at your expense, to engage the services of a qualified specialist to inspect the Property for the presence of wetlands prior to submitting a written offer to purchase the Property or you may include in your written offer, subject to the Seller's acceptance, a clause making your purchase of the Property contingent upon a satisfactory wetlands inspection.

36. HOMEOWNERS ASSOCIATION: The Property is not part of a development subject to the imposition of mandatory fees as defined by the Maryland Homeowners Association Act, unless acknowledged by attached addendum.

37. FOREIGN INVESTMENT TAXES-FIRPTA: Section 1445 of the United States Internal Revenue Code of 1986 provides that a buyer of a residential real property located in the United States must withhold federal income taxes from the payment of the purchase price if (a) the purchase price exceeds Three Hundred Thousand Dollars ($300,000.00) and (b) the seller is a foreign person. Unless otherwise stated in an addendum attached hereto, if the purchase price is in excess of Three Hundred Thousand Dollars ($300,000.00), Seller represents that Seller is not a non-resident alien, foreign corporation, foreign partnership, foreign trust or foreign estate (as those terms are defined by the Internal Revenue Code and applicable regulations) and agrees to execute an affidavit to this effect at the time of settlement.

38. AGRICULTURALLY ASSESSED PROPERTY: The Property, or any portion thereof, may be subject to an "Agricultural Land Transfer Tax" as imposed by Section 13-301 et seq. of the Tax-Property Article of the Annotated Code of Maryland by reason of the Property having been assessed on the basis of agricultural use. The additional tax shall be paid by Buyer unless otherwise negotiated.

39. INTERNAL REVENUE SERVICE FILING: Buyer and Seller each agree to cooperate with the person responsible for settlement by providing all necessary information so that a report can be filed with the Internal Revenue Service, as required by Section 6045 of the IRS Code. To the extent permitted by law, any fees incurred as a result of such filing will be paid by the Seller.

Figure 11.1   Maryland Association of REALTORS® Residential Sales Contract (Page 5 of 5)

40. GUARANTY FUND: NOTICE TO BUYER, THE BUYER IS PROTECTED BY THE REAL ESTATE GUARANTY FUND OF THE MARYLAND REAL ESTATE COMMISSION FOR LOSSES COVERED BY SECTION 17-404 OF THE BUSINESS OCCUPATIONS AND PROFESSIONS ARTICLE OF THE MARYLAND CODE, IN AN AMOUNT NOT EXCEEDING $25,000 FOR ANY CLAIM.

41. HOME AND/OR ENVIRONMENTAL INSPECTION: Buyer acknowledges, subject to Seller acceptance, that Buyer is afforded the opportunity, at Buyer's sole cost and expense, to condition Buyer's purchase of the Property upon a Home Inspection and/or Environmental Inspection in order to ascertain the physical condition of the Property or the existence of environmental hazards. If Buyer desires a Home Inspection and/or Environmental Inspection contingency, such contingency must be included in an Addendum to this Contract at the time it is signed by Buyer. Buyer acknowledges that neither the Brokers, their agents or subagents are responsible for property defects.

Addenda Attached _____   Inspections Declined _____
              Buyer's Initials   *Buyer's Initials*

42. LEAD-BASED PAINT HAZARDS: Title X, Section 1018, the Residential Lead-Based Paint Hazard Reduction Act of 1992 (the Act), requires the disclosure of certain information regarding lead-based paint and lead-based paint hazards in connection with the sale of residential real property. Unless otherwise exempt, the Act applies only to housing constructed prior to 1978. A Seller of pre-1978 housing is required to disclose to the Buyer(s), based upon the Seller's actual knowledge, all known lead-based paint hazards in the Property and provide the Buyer(s) with any available reports in the Seller's possession relating to lead-based paint or lead-based paint hazards applicable to the Property. The Seller, however, is not required to conduct or pay for any lead-based paint risk assessment or inspection. At the time that the offer to purchase is entered into by the Buyer(s), the Seller is required to provide the Buyer(s) with the EPA pamphlet entitled "Protect Your Family From Lead In Your Home" and a "Disclosure of Information on Lead -Based Paint and Lead-Based Paint Hazards" form.

The Seller is required under the Act to provide the Buyer(s) with a ten (10) day time period (or other mutually agreeable time period) for the Buyer(s), at Buyer's expense, to conduct a risk assessment or inspection for the presence of lead-based paint and/or lead-based paint hazards unless the Buyer(s) waives such assessment or inspection by indicating such waiver on the Lead-Based Paint Disclosure form. Seller and any agent involved in the transaction are required to retain a copy of the completed Lead-Based Paint Disclosure form for a period of three (3) years following the date of settlement. The Act became effective September 6, 1996, for a Seller who owns more than four (4) dwelling units, whether single-family or multi-family, and December 6, 1996, for a Seller who owns four (4) or fewer dwelling units.

A SELLER WHO FAILS TO GIVE THE REQUIRED LEAD-BASED PAINT DISCLOSURE FORM AND EPA PAMPHLET MAY BE LIABLE UNDER THE ACT FOR THREE TIMES THE AMOUNT OF DAMAGES AND MAY BE SUBJECT TO BOTH CIVIL AND CRIMINAL PENALTIES.

Seller represents and warrants to Buyer, Broker(s), Brokers' agents and subagents, intending that they rely upon such warranty and representation, that the property: (Seller to initial applicable line): _____ was constructed prior to 1978 OR _____ was not constructed prior to 1978 OR _____ the date of construction is uncertain. If the Property was constructed prior to 1978 or if the date of construction is uncertain, as indicated by Seller's initial above, Seller and Buyer mutually agree that the requirements of the Act shall apply to the sale of the Property. Seller and Buyer acknowledge that the real estate brokers and salespersons involved in the sale of the Property have no duty to ascertain or verify the date of construction and assume no such duty or responsibility. Seller and Buyer agree and represent and warrant, each unto the other, that no binding and enforceable contract shall be deemed to exist or to have been formed unless the requirements of the Act have been complied with prior to the execution of this Contract by Seller and Buyer. Seller and Buyer represent and warrant that each intended, as a material term of the offer and acceptance, that the requirements of the Act be complied with as an express condition of the formation of a binding and enforceable contract by and between the parties. Buyer and Seller acknowledge by their respective initials below that they have read and understand the provisions of this Paragraph 42.

              Buyer's Initials   *Seller's Initials*

43. ADDENDA: The Addenda checked below which bear the signatures of all parties which are hereby attached and made a part of this Contract and shall be construed to govern over any inconsistent portions of this printed form (check applicable boxes):

☐ Affiliated Business Disclosure Notice
☐ Condominium Resale
☐ Disclosure of Licensee Status
☐ First-Time Maryland Home Buyer Transfer & Recordation Tax Addendum
☐ Homeowners Association
☐ Inspection - Environmental
☐ Inspection - Home
☐ Inspection - Radon

☐ Inspection/Certification - Septic
☐ Inspection/Certification - Well
☐ Lead-Based Paint Hazard Inspection
☐ Lead-Based Paint and Lead-Based Hazards Disclosure of Information
☐ Local City/County Certifications/Registrations
☐ Local City/County Notices/Disclosures
☐ Notice to Buyer - Rights Under Maryland Seller Disclosure/Disclaimer Act

☐ Post Settlement Occupancy Agreement
☐ Pre-Settlement Occupancy Agreement
☐ Private Maintenance Agreement
☐ Removal (Kickout) of Contingency
☐ Sale, Settlement or Lease of Other Real Estate
☐ Seller's Purchase of Another Property
☐ Third Party Approval
☐ Other Addenda/Special Conditions (specify below)

44. PARAGRAPH HEADINGS: The Paragraph headings of this Contract are for convenience and reference only, and in no way define or limit the intent, rights or obligations of the parties.

45. ENTIRE AGREEMENT: This Contract and any Addenda thereto contain the final and entire agreement between the parties, and neither they nor their agents shall be bound by any terms, conditions, statements, warranties or representations, oral or written, not herein contained. The parties to this Contract mutually agree that it is binding upon them, their heirs, executors, administrators, personal representatives, successors and, if permitted as herein provided, assigns. Once signed, the terms of this Contract can only be changed by a document executed by all parties. This Contract shall be interpreted and construed in accordance with the laws of the State of Maryland. It is further agreed that this Contract may be executed in counterparts, each of which when considered together shall constitute the original contract.

46. ELECTRONIC DELIVERY: The parties agree that this Contract offer shall be deemed validly executed and delivered by a party if a party executes this Contract and delivers a copy of the executed Contract to the other party by telefax or telecopier transmittal.

(PLEASE SIGN THE ORIGINAL AND ALL COPIES INDIVIDUALLY)

_____   _____ (SEAL)
          Buyer's Signature   **Date**

_____   _____ (SEAL)
          Buyer's Signature   **Date**

_____   _____ (SEAL)
          Seller's Signature   **Date**

_____   _____ (SEAL)
          Seller's Signature   **Date**

DATE OF CONTRACT ACCEPTANCE: _____

QUESTIONS

1. In Maryland, contracts for the sale of real estate must be

   a. in writing to be enforceable.
   b. on a standard printed form.
   c. signed by the seller only.
   d. signed by the buyer only.

2. Oral contracts for the sale of real estate are

   a. valid.
   b. called *parol* agreements.
   c. enforceable in a court of law.
   d. illegal.

3. Licensees buying or selling real property must

   a. advise the other party of their licensee status.
   b. advise lending institutions of their status.
   c. write to the Real Estate Commission.
   d. advise the Attorney General.

4. Which of the following disclosures will NOT be necessary in a Maryland real estate sales contract?

   a. That a leasehold interest is involved in the sale
   b. That the seller is a real estate licensee
   c. The existence of possible tax charges for agricultural land development
   d. The name of the title insurance company

5. Absent instructions to the contrary from their owner and beneficial owner, the Brokers Act states that earnest money deposits

   a. may be commingled with the broker's funds.
   b. must be deposited in an insured and approved financial institution in Maryland.
   c. are to be placed in an interest-bearing account.
   d. may be withdrawn at any time prior to settlement as long as a licensee's signature appears on the escrow check.

12

Transfer of Title

OVERVIEW

Title to land in Maryland, as elsewhere, can pass by descent, devise, adverse possession, gift, escheat, eminent domain, erosion, foreclosure and tax and sheriff's sales.

TRANSFER OF TITLE BY DESCENT

Maryland has eliminated the rights of dower and curtesy discussed in Chapter 7 of the main text in favor of the Maryland Law of Descent and Distribution. This law names the classes of heirs who inherit real estate owned by a deceased owner who dies **intestate**, that is, without leaving a valid will. In such cases, the surviving spouse is always an heir, as are children of the deceased. All distributions are made after payment of the decedent's debts and estate taxes.

TRANSFER OF TITLE BY ACTION OF LAW

To obtain title to real estate through **adverse possession**, an adverse user must be in actual possession of the property, and that possession, alone or combined with that of previous adverse owners, must have been continuous for 20 years. The possession also must be or have been open, notorious, exclusive and hostile, and—because Maryland law does not recognize "squatters' rights"—under claim of right or color of title (with each of those terms having a very specific legal meaning). Situations involving adverse possession require guidance of legal counsel.

TRANSFER OF TITLE BY WILL

There are statutory **requirements for a valid will**. A person aged 18 or over who is of sound mind and is legally competent may make a will. Wills should be prepared carefully by the testator's attorney and signed and witnessed as required by law. While surviving spouses can contest wills that grant them less than their intestate share, testators' children do not have this right.

TRANSFER OF TITLE BY DEED

Statutes also set **requirements for a valid deed**. A deed must be in writing, executed by a competent grantor 18 years of age or older, state a consideration, and give a legally sufficient property description. The deed must either show the actual consideration or be accompanied by an affidavit that states it. Although unrecorded deeds are valid between grantors and grantees, to protect grantees against third parties, deeds must be recorded. Recordation requires acknowledgment before a notary or other authorized public officer.

Transfers of property belonging to a minor and those involving corporate sellers or purchasers are situations in which the grantee as well as the grantor is required to sign the deed.

Maryland law specifies that the transfer of any fee or freehold estate, any declaration or limitation of use and any estate extending beyond seven years (such as a lease) shall be effective only if the deed is executed and recorded.

Deeds must be typewritten and in English to be recorded, although an accompanying official consular translation into English satisfies this requirement for a deed recorded in another language.

TAXES ON CONVEYANCES

The **documentary stamp tax** (so-called because its payment until several decades ago was witnessed by attaching actual revenue stamps to the deed) is a Maryland state tax levied at the rate of $.55 per $500 or fraction thereof on the full sales price of the property. Several cities and counties have added their own stamp tax. Another state tax is the Maryland **transfer tax**. It is one-half of 1 percent of the full consideration paid for the property sold, except

for transfers to a first-time Maryland home buyer, as explained in Chapter 10 of this volume. Several cities and counties collect an additional transfer tax.

AGRICULTURAL TRANSFER TAX

Any transfer of land not subject to the provisions of the former development tax is subject to the agricultural transfer tax, which is calculated by the Assessments Office and is payable at the time of property transfer.

The agricultural transfer tax will be levied when these conditions in transactions involving land transfers occur:

- Whenever the property sold represents land only, the tax shall be computed on the total consideration if the property has been assessed solely on the basis of agricultural use, but it will be computed on the net consideration if the property has been assessed on the basis of a combined agricultural and nonagricultural use. The net consideration is the total price paid less the most recent full cash value on the non-agriculturally assessed portion.
- Whenever the property has been assessed on the basis of both an agricultural use and a nonagricultural use, including structures, the tax shall be computed on the net consideration.
- Whenever the transaction comprises individual building lots of fewer than 20 acres that did not receive the combined agricultural use and the nonagricultural use assessment,

the tax shall be imposed on the total consideration.

The agricultural transfer tax rate is

- 5 percent when the land being transferred is a parcel of 20 acres or more;
- 4 percent when the land is a parcel of fewer than 20 acres and is assessed on the basis of its agricultural use or on the basis of unimproved land;
- 3 percent when the land is a parcel of fewer than 20 acres and is assessed as improved land or land with site improvements; or
- reduced by 25 percent for each consecutive full taxable year in which real property taxes were paid on the basis of a nonagricultural use assessment.

When a buyer files a **Declaration of Intent** to keep the land being transferred in agricultural use for at least five full consecutive taxable years, and provided the property otherwise meets the qualifications for an agricultural use assessment, the tax is deferred until the next sale of the property occurs. If the buyer fails to adhere to the stipulations contained in the Declaration of Intent, the rate of the tax does not decrease until taxes based on nonagricultural use have been paid for five years.

STATE TRANSFER TAX EXEMPTIONS

The state transfer tax does not apply to the recordation of any instrument that transfers an interest in property to an organization that the Department of Assessments and Taxation has certified as meeting all of the following requirements:

- Is exempt from federal income taxation
- Is incorporated in Maryland or, if not, is registered to do business in Maryland
- Has as its principal purpose the preservation of agricultural land, including temporary ownership of interests in land for the purpose of preservation of its character as agricultural land

Mortgages or deeds of trust are exempt from the recordation tax if they secure home equity **loans made for the initial purchase or for renovation** of one's residence.

Transfers between relatives, including in-laws and former spouses, are exempt from recordation and transfer taxes only on the mortgage or deed of trust indebtedness assumed by the transferee.

Special rules apply to taxing leases that create a perpetually renewable **ground rent** with or without transfer of the reversionary estate.

MARYLAND UNIFORM TRANSFERS TO MINORS ACT

This law authorizes a donor to nominate a nonliable custodian to act on behalf of a minor beneficiary. The designation, powers and responsibilities of a custodian and procedures for transfers of custodial property and claims against such property are set forth in the statute.

QUESTIONS

1. One requirement for obtaining title to the property of another by adverse possession is that the claimant must

    a. post a sign on the subject property.
    b. notify the original owner in writing.
    c. be in possession of the property for 20 years.
    d. own the adjoining land.

2. The Maryland Law of Descent and Distribution

    a. can apply to the estates of those not leaving a valid will.
    b. assures surviving spouses part of any estate.
    c. can apply to estates of those leaving a valid will.
    d. All the above

3. To be valid between the parties, a deed to Maryland real property must meet all the following requirements EXCEPT that it be

    a. voluntarily delivered during the lifetime of the grantor.
    b. in writing and signed.
    c. signed by a grantor who is competent.
    d. recorded.

4. To be eligible for recordation, a deed

    a. need only show a nominal consideration.
    b. must be in the handwriting of the grantee.
    c. must have been prepared by an attorney or by one of the parties.
    d. must be witnessed by two persons not mentioned in the deed.

13

Title Records

OVERVIEW

According to Maryland state law, deeds, mortgages, ground leases and other instruments creating an estate in real estate for longer than seven years must be recorded to be enforceable against third parties. This serves to protect lessees against such third parties as lenders, judgment creditors, etc. In the purchase of real property, the grantee is responsible for recording the deed and paying recording fees.

The law requires subdividers to record plats of subdivision after their approval by state and local authorities. Later documents such as listings, sales contracts and deeds can refer to the recorded plats by liber and folio (book and page). Such reference in a later document satisfies the need for exact property description.

DETAILS OF RECORDATION

To be eligible for recordation, a deed must state the full, actual **consideration** paid for the property; if the information is not in the deed, it must be stated in an affidavit attached to the deed.

Deeds and mortgages of real estate are **recorded by the circuit court clerk** of each county and Baltimore City. Recording must take place **in the county or city where the land is located**. If property is located in two counties, it must be recorded in both, with each county receiving a recording fee proportional to the amount of land located in the county, as shown by the tax assessment. Occasionally recordings are made in a county other than that in which the property is located. It should be noted that Maryland has only one system of recording. The Torrens system, as described in the main text, does not exist in Maryland.

Real estate records are indexed by the names of the **grantor and grantee**. All references to a previously recorded conveyance should give not only the liber (book) and folio (page) numbers where the conveyance is found but also the name of the grantor and the grantee who were parties to the conveyance. Purchasers who finance a property purchased with a purchase-money mortgage or deed of trust to a financial institution are the grantees named in their own deed. They will then become grantors shown in the deed of trust they give to a financial institution. In the first instance, their names will be recorded in the grantee index; in the second, in the grantor index.

No deed conveying real estate may be recorded in any county of Maryland until all **taxes and other public assessments** or charges on the property have been paid and the record of ownership has been transferred on the tax assessment books to the grantee who is named in the deed to be recorded. If the deed transfers all of the real estate owned by the grantor in the county, then, in many counties, all of the grantor's personal property tax must also be paid prior to recording.

In Baltimore City, a deed conveying real estate may not be recorded if there is an **unpaid water bill** over $50. In Harford County, no deed conveying real estate may be recorded unless the water bill is paid. Requirements should be checked in the county or municipality involved.

The amount of **fees charged for the recording** of deeds and other documents is set by counties. In many counties it is $3 per page, or portion thereof, plus $1 for each name to be recorded in the grantor-grantee index. One who records a document takes it to the court clerk's office, pays the proper amount of documentary stamps and transfer tax stamps, pays the recording fee and leaves the document with the clerk. The clerk's staff then reproduces the document in the public record, stamps it to indicate where the information has been recorded and returns it to the person designated to receive it.

REAL ESTATE BROKERS AND SUBDIVISION LAWS REGARDING RECORDING

Recordation and development of individual lots in a subdivision are regulated on a local level by the county in which the property is located. Licensees should always be sure that the deeds to the individual lots for sale in a subdivision have been properly recorded and that all local laws regarding recordation have been met before advertising the lots for sale. Failure to do so could result in a judicial injunction, which would halt the marketing of the property. In addition, depending on the situation, the licensees may also be in violation of the state license law and subject to suspension or revocation of their real estate licenses.

TITLE EVIDENCE

In Maryland, it is customary for buyers in a real estate transaction to obtain and pay for title evidence. Generally, they will hire attorneys who will usually do one of two things: (1) have an abstract of title prepared and, based on the abstract, prepare a certificate of title indicating their professional opinion of the present condition of the title or (2) acting as licensed representatives of a title insurance company, personally issue a title insurance policy binder based on examination of the abstract. The attorneys will either deliver this abstract to the purchaser or forward it to the title insurance company so that the company may issue a title policy. The person performing settlement must explain owner's title insurance and make it available to the purchasers.

Note that Maryland law requires that the following notice be given to buyers, printed in bold type in the body of each sales contract presented by licensees: YOU ARE ENTITLED TO SELECT YOUR OWN TITLE INSURANCE COMPANY, SETTLEMENT COMPANY, ESCROW COMPANY OR TITLE ATTORNEY.

PREREQUISITES TO RECORDING

No fee simple deed, mortgage or deed of trust may be recorded unless it bears a certification that the instrument has been prepared by attorneys admitted to practice before the Maryland Court of Appeals or under the supervision of such attorneys, or by one of the parties to the instrument. There are other requirements imposed by various localities.

UNIFORM COMMERCIAL CODE

The Uniform Commercial Code (UCC) is in effect in Maryland. Two provisions of this code may affect real estate practices. The use of chattel mortgages on fixtures or contents has been replaced by use of security agreements and financing statements. The bulk sales provision applies when a person sells all of the stock in trade when selling a business. The main text contains more information about the UCC.

QUESTIONS

1. Buyers purchased a parcel of real estate that is located in two counties. They should record in

   a. the county with the larger portion.
   b. the county with the smaller portion.
   c. the State capital.
   d. both counties.

2. When a parcel of Maryland real estate is sold, title search is usually ordered by the

   a. seller.
   b. buyer.
   c. broker.
   d. seller and broker together.

3. Deeds and mortgages may be recorded in each county with the

   a. circuit court clerk.
   b. Torrens system.
   c. tax office.
   d. office of planning and zoning.

4. In Maryland, county real estate records are NOT

   a. indexed under the name of the grantor.
   b. indexed under the name of the grantee.
   c. indexed under the name of the selling broker.
   d. referenced to previously recorded conveyances.

Real Estate Financing

OVERVIEW

Most real estate is purchased using borrowed funds. Both the traditional mortgage and the **deed of trust** are common in Maryland and are used both in third-party and in owner financing. The State allows, but stringently regulates, another form of owner financing—the installment land contract.

NOTE TO STUDENT

The deed **of** trust—also called a *trust deed*—is different from a deed **in** trust, which is used to place property into a trust. Both are different from a *trustee's deed* by which property is transferred out of a trust by the trustee.

MORTGAGE AND DEED OF TRUST LOANS

Maryland is considered a **title theory** state as defined in the main text. A lender who records a properly signed and delivered mortgage or deed of trust holds legal title to the real estate pledged. Maryland's mortgage and deed of trust foreclosure and sale laws, however, are similar to those of a **lien theory** state. Deeds of trust are widely used throughout the state as financing instruments for real estate. The standard FHLMC/FNMA loan forms simplify the packaging and selling of such loans in the secondary market, as discussed in the text.

Deed of trust financing is a three-party arrangement involving borrower (the trustor), trustee and lender (beneficiary). Under the deed of trust forms used in Maryland, the **power of sale clause** gives the trustee authority to sell pledged property in the event of borrower's default. In such a case, there is no court action. After giving adequate public notice, the trustee has the property sold at trustee sale—a public auction.

The money the trustee obtains from the sale is then applied to the principal of the mortgage debt plus the accrued interest and legal costs caused by the sale. Any money left, over and above what is due any lienholder, is returned to the defaulted borrower.

In Maryland, only a natural person and not a corporation or partnership may serve under a deed of trust and sell the property in case of default under the provisions of the document's power-of-sale clause. In some other jurisdictions any person, including corporations and partnerships, may serve.

DEFAULT, FORECLOSURE, AND DEFICIENCY

The parties to a mortgage are the mortgagor (borrower) and the mortgagee (lender). If the borrower defaults, the lender who wishes to foreclose seeks a court order to sell the mortgaged property at public auction, unless there is a power of sale clause in the mortgage. When the funds from a judicial (court-ordered) mortgage foreclosure sale are insufficient to satisfy the debt, a judgment may be issued against the borrower for the deficiency. However when a deficiency occurs after a non-judicial foreclosure either by a trustee or by the mortgagee under a power-of-sale clause, no such judgment is entered. Deficiency actions are not allowed in **Federal Housing Administration** (FHA)loans, and the **Department of Veterans Affairs (DVA)** is reluctant to allow them.

INTEREST RATES AND USURY

In Maryland, there is no limit on the rate of interest a lender may charge a borrower in first mortgage loans. The written agreement between mortgagor and mortgagee must specify the rate of interest and cannot require any prepayment penalty. However, the agreement can require a prepayment penalty of no more than two months' interest in the event the interest rate is 8 percent or less and the borrower pays off the mortgage during the first three years of the loan. The state interest ceiling on second mortgage loans and land installment contracts is 24 percent.

Violators of the state usury law face penalties requiring the lender to forfeit an amount equal to three times the interest charges collected over the permissible amount or $500, whichever is greater, and pay court costs.

MORTGAGE EXPENSE ACCOUNTS

Maryland savings institutions that require a tax and insurance **expense**—also called *escrow* or *impound*—**account** for mortgage and deed of trust loans must pay interest on these funds at passbook rate, but not less than 3 percent. The interest is computed on the average monthly balance in the escrow account and paid annually by crediting the borrower's account with the amount of interest due. This payment is reported to the IRS on a form 1099. Loans sold to agencies in the secondary mortgage market are exempt from this requirement.

DISCRIMINATION

Under Maryland law, a lender may not refuse loans to any person based solely on geographic area, neighborhood, race, creed, color, age, sex, disability, marital status, familial status or national origin. However, a lender may refuse loans based on higher-than-normal risks connected with the loan.

GROUND RENT—FHA/DVA LOANS

The Department of Veterans Affairs will guarantee loans only on properties that are subject to ground rent located only in Anne Arundel County, Baltimore City, Baltimore County and the Joppatowne subdivision in Harford County. If a veteran purchases leasehold property located in another part of the state using such financing—often called a "GI" loan—the ground rent must be redeemed on or prior to the date of closing. For Federal Housing Administration (FHA) loans on Maryland property held subject to a ground rent, the residential mortgage limit must be reduced by the capitalization value of the annual ground rent. Ground rents are discussed in Chapter 16 of this volume.

RELEASE OF MORTGAGE LIEN

When a mortgage note has been fully repaid by the borrower, the lender must release the lien of the mortgage. This may be done by a separate form referred to as a **satisfaction of mortgage** or a **deed of release**. If a deed of trust form is used, a separate form of release may be recorded to clear the borrower's title.

In some instances, the mortgagee simply enters the statement of release directly in the margin of the recorded mortgage; then the mortgage form is re-recorded so that the public record will indicate the release. Recording of the release provides public notice that the original mortgage lien has been canceled.

MORTGAGE PRESUMED PAID

A mortgage or deed of trust will be presumed to have been paid and the lien created by that document removed if 12 years have elapsed since the last payment (maturity) date called for in the instrument. Alternatively, if that date cannot be ascertained and 40 years have elapsed since the date of the document's recording, the mortgage will be presumed paid and the lien extinguished.

FORECLOSURE-TRUSTEE SALE

The mortgage or deed of trust—but not the note—must be recorded before a lender may start foreclosure proceedings in case of borrower default. State law requires that in order to record a residential mortgage or deed of trust, a lender must execute and attach an affidavit to each mortgage stating (1) that the mortgage document accurately sets forth the amount of the loan and (2) that the entire amount was disbursed when the mortgage was executed or delivered to the lender by the borrower.

When a mortgage does not contain a provision giving the mortgagee the power of sale, a foreclosure sale ordered and supervised by the court is the lender's final remedy for default by the borrower. Because there is no statutory period provided for redemption of property *after* foreclosure sale, a defaulted borrower has to make redemption by paying the necessary funds to the mortgagee *before* the sale has been completed—that is, before the court officer delivers the sale deed to the purchaser. Mortgagees or trustees are permitted to personally purchase properties in default at the sale rather than sell them to satisfy debts, provided they have diligently attempted to obtain the best possible price for each property on the market.

Holders of subordinate interests in real property may record a request for a notice of sale, requiring holders of superior interests in property to give notice of an impending foreclosure sale. They must file this **surplus money action** to receive any of the proceeds of a scheduled foreclosure sale. If holders of such junior liens fail to do this, their liens will be extinguished, no matter how large the proceeds from the sale.

Annual crops planted or cultivated by the mortgagor do not pass with property sold under a foreclosure sale unless so stated in the mortgage or deed of trust; such crops remain the property of the debtor. After the sale, an agreement may be reached on a reasonable rental of that part of the property occupied by the crops. This rental becomes a lien on the crops and continues until paid. If the parties cannot agree on such rental, it may be determined by the courts.

Note that foreclosure sale under a deed of trust or mortgage in default may terminate any leaseholds on the property that began after the deed of trust was executed and recorded. Leaseholds entered into before the date of the mortgage may survive if they meet any requirements for recordation of leases longer than seven years. Tenants whose leases contain subordination agreements or who have later granted such agreements will not be protected. Strict foreclosure, as described in the text, is not recognized in Maryland.

LAND INSTALLMENT CONTRACTS

The state law regarding land installment contract sales of real estate is found in the Annotated Code of Maryland, *Real Property Article*, at Title 10. Note that this law applies only to the sale of improved properties, occupied or to be occupied by the purchaser as a dwelling, or of an unimproved, subdivided lot or lots intended to be improved for residential purposes. Land installment contracts should be prepared and processed by attorneys. The purchaser may rescind the contract and demand that all sums paid be returned if the vendor does not record the contract within 15 days of its being signed by all parties. Land installment contract financing also requires cumbersome ongoing processing by the vendor designed to protect the purchaser. As stated earlier, the maximum interest rate allowed by Maryland statute on land contracts is 24 percent.

JUNIOR FINANCING

The maximum interest rate a lender may charge in Maryland for a second mortgage is 24 percent; the maximum loan origination fee that may be charged is two points, out of which are paid all costs such as appraisal fee and credit report. Only an actual cost, such as a recording fee or title insurance, may be charged over the two-point fee. A junior loan may be refinanced no more than once in every 12-month period and not more than twice during any five-year period. The *Commercial Law Article* of the Maryland Annotated Code sets forth the details.

Junior lenders in Maryland are prohibited from certain practices, including the following:

- Attempting to have the debtor waive his or her legal rights
- Requiring accelerated payments, except in case of default
- Having the debtor execute an assignment of wages for payment of the loan
- Charging a fee to execute a release after the loan is paid

BALLOON PAYMENTS

As revised in 1984, the Maryland Secondary Mortgage Law requires private individuals who take back a second mortgage with a balloon clause to grant, upon the borrower's request, an automatic, one-time, six-month extension to the maturity date. The law also permits all fees, discounts and points allowed or required under federally related second mortgage purchase programs. However, the points and interest rate computed together may not exceed an annual percentage rate (APR) of 24 percent.

RESIDENTIAL PROPERTY LOAN NOTICES

Lenders who make loans on residential property are required to provide prospective borrowers with a written notice informing them of their right to choose an attorney or a title insurance company. This notice must be provided within three days of their application for the loan. They are also required to notify applicants that by completing their loan applications, they are terminating any right they might have had to rescind the contract for lack of a Property Disclosure/Disclaimer statement.

QUESTIONS

1. Mortgages on Maryland real property

   a. must be recorded to be valid between lender and borrower.
   b. may not be refused to any persons because of their religion.
   c. by law must be for a minimum ten-year term.
   d. may be foreclosed by strict foreclosure if in default.

2. In Maryland, a land installment contract need NOT

   a. be recorded by the vendor within 15 days after it has been signed.
   b. include all terms of the transaction.
   c. be signed by the vendor and vendee.
   d. be filed with the Real Estate Commission.

3. The DVA will guarantee a loan on real property in Maryland that is held subject to a ground rent

   a. only in certain areas of the State.
   b. and the loan limit must be reduced by the capitalized value of the annual rent.
   c. only to the in-fee value of the property.
   d. only in Baltimore City.

4. Peter Arnett obtains a loan to purchase a new home from BNN Savings Bank. BNN fails to record the mortgage document. The mortgage does not give BNN the power of sale in case of default. Which of the following is true?

   a. As things stand, BNN Savings Bank will be able to enforce the mortgage in a court of law if Arnett defaults on his loan.
   b. If Arnett defaults on the loan, BNN cannot foreclose on the mortgage in court until the instrument is recorded.
   c. As mortgagor, it is Arnett's obligation to record the mortgage for his own protection.
   d. If Arnett defaults on the loan, BNN could sell the property without foreclosure action.

5. Jay-Cee Hayward obtains a 30-year loan from Liberty Savings Association to purchase a Baltimore condominium unit. Along with monthly payments of principal and interest, the lender requires Hayward to deposit funds in an escrow account for the payment of taxes and property insurance. Which of the following is true?

   a. Liberty Savings must pay Hayward interest on these escrow deposits when the loan is paid off.
   b. Hayward may require the lender to maintain her escrow account in an interest-bearing depository.
   c. Liberty Savings must credit Hayward's account for passbook rate interest on her escrow deposits annually.
   d. Hayward must pay the lender a minimum of 3 percent interest for maintaining such an account for her.

6. George Michael needs $165,000 to purchase a new home, and he borrows it from First Maryland Savings Bank. Which of the following security arrangements may First Maryland SB use?

   a. Mortgage or deed of trust
   b. Real estate trust
   c. Installment contract
   d. Deed of release

16

Leases

OVERVIEW

Leaseholds in Maryland are the four familiar common law estates: leases for a specified time period ("for years"), leases from period to period ("from year to year"), tenancies at will, and tenancies at sufferance. Long-term ground leases, an example of the first type, are common in certain areas.

MARYLAND GROUND RENTS

Ground leases exist in several areas in the State. Some of them may be redeemed after specified time periods, while others are irredeemable. The ground lease tenant typically owns the improvements located on the rented ground.

Ground rental is money paid to the landowner (landlord) by a tenant who possesses the landlord's land by virtue of a lease. Such leases usually give tenants possession of land for specific time periods up to 99 years. Possession of the land reverts to the fee simple land owner when the lease finally expires, if it is terminated by the tenant's default, or if it is not renewed. Many such agreements have options for renewal for additional time periods either at predetermined graduated rentals or for rentals to be based on reappraisal of the land and improvements at the time of renewal.

Any leasehold interest can be sold, mortgaged, assigned and subleased. When tenants sell leaseholds, they assign their possessory rights to the purchaser in a document that clearly says that the estate being conveyed is less than a freehold and is, therefore, regarded as personal property rather than real property.

Creation of a Ground Rent

Anyone who owns unencumbered fee simple property can subject the property to ground rent, thus creating a leasehold estate. The worth of the reversion is based on the capitalization value of the ground rent. Although any amount of ground rental can be charged for a property, the rent typically is reasonable to make the property marketable. Ground rent amounts are usually based on rents charged for comparable lots (competitive rents) in the neighborhood or simply "what the market will bear." The student should be aware that capitalization of the annual ground rent amount does not necessarily represent the true value of the piece of land. (Capitalization of rent or income is discussed in the following section.)

The expenses involved in originating or creating a new ground rent include charges for recording the lease, Maryland revenue stamps and transfer tax based on the capitalized value, notary fees and legal fees for drawing the lease.

Redemption of Certain Residential Ground Rents

Leases executed before April 9, 1884, are irredeemable. Some of those ground rents are still in existence today, if they were renewed. However, many ground leases made after that date may be redeemed at the costs and the times shown below.

The *Real Property Article* of the Maryland statutes provides that leases of residential land (except apartment and cooperative leases) for periods of longer than 15 years are redeemable at the option of the tenant. This means that tenants may purchase the rented land in fee simple from their ground landlords. Note that this redemption right does not apply to commercial, industrial, mercantile or manufacturing property.

They can do this by giving their landlords one month's notice and then paying them a sum of money equal to the capitalization of the annual rental at rates that do not exceed those shown below:

- For leases written between April 9, 1884, and April 5, 1888, capitalize the annual rental by dividing it by 4 percent (.04).
- If the lease was created, or is being created, after July 1, 1982, compute the cost of capitalization by dividing the annual rental by 12 percent (.12).
- If the lease was created at any other time, capitalize the annual rental by dividing it by 6 percent (.06).

For example, if the annual rental on a residential lot under ground rent is $240, and the capitalization rate is 12 percent, the cost to redeem the property by capitalizing it would be $2,000.

Rationale: $240 ÷ .12 = $2,000

Redemption may be for any lesser sum specified in the lease or for another sum to which the parties may agree at the time of redemption.

The time at which **notice to redeem** can be given is dictated by the date on which the leases were created. For example: For a lease executed before July 1, 1969, notice to redeem can be given at any time; if executed between July 1, 1969, and July 1, 1971, at the end of five years from date of lease; if executed between July 1, 1971, and July 1, 1982, at the end of three years from date of lease; if executed on or after July 1, 1982, at the end of five years from date of lease.

Ground Rent Disclosure

When property is sold subject to ground rent, the law requires the seller to give the buyer notice of this ground rent at the time of settlement. The seller must further inform the new leaseholder that nonpayment of the ground rent may result in reversion of the entire property to the ground landlord. Licensees posting signs announcing property for sale that is already subject to ground rent are required to show on the sign the amount of annual ground rental in numbers as large and clear as the numbers showing the price of the property.

If a contract of sale of property subject to ground rent does not disclose the ground rent and calls for delivery of fee simple title to the purchaser, the seller must redeem the property before settlement. If the property is irredeemable, the seller cannot deliver fee simple title and will be in breach of contract.

MARYLAND RESIDENTIAL LEASES

In the *Real Property Article*, the Maryland Statute of Frauds provides that, to be enforceable, leases for a year or less need not be in writing. Those whose term is more than one year must be written. The time periods are measured from "the inception of a lease"—the date the instrument is signed—until the end of its term.

Leases longer than seven years must be **recorded**. Recordation requires acknowledgment before a notary public or similar official. Note, however, that even when such leases have not been properly recorded, they are still valid and binding between the original parties, against their creditors and against their successors and assignees who have actual notice of the lease or who acquire the property when a tenant is in actual occupancy.

Possession of the property by a tenant under a lease for seven years or less gives **constructive notice** of the tenant's rights.

Although the law requires any lease for a term longer than seven years to be recorded, a *memorandum of lease* may be recorded instead.

Disclosure of representation. Representation of either lessor or lessee must be disclosed to the other party in negotiation of all residential leases that are for more than 125 days. The disclosure must be made to prospective tenants or prospective landlords, whichever may apply, no later than their first scheduled meeting with a licensee. Please review the discussion on disclosure of representation in Chapter 4/5 of this volume.

An **application for a lease** must contain a statement explaining the liabilities incurred by the tenant upon signing the application, including the tenant's obligation to take possession if the application is accepted. If the landlord requires any fees other than a security deposit—perhaps a credit check to verify information in the application—and these fees exceed $25, the landlord is required to return the fees in excess of the actual amount spent. This applies to landlords who offer five or more rental units on one parcel of property but not to seasonal rentals or condominiums.

Landlords may not require **security deposits** of more than two months' rent or $50, whichever is more. The landlord must give the tenant a receipt for the deposit. Failure to do so makes the landlord liable to the tenant for the sum of $25. Deposit monies must be placed and maintained by brokers in an account maintained for this sole purpose in a Maryland banking or savings institution within 30 days of receipt. Affiliates of brokers deliver any such monies that come into their possession into the hands of their brokers for prompt deposit into the brokers' accounts. Broker licensees' records of these funds must be available for inspection by members of the Commission or its agents during normal business hours.

At the time leases are written, landlords must give tenants written notice of tenants' right, within 15 days of the beginning of the lease, to demand from landlords a written property condition report. A landlord who fails to provide this report to tenants who make the proper request becomes liable to the tenants for three times the amount of any security deposit. This amount could be reduced (offset) by amounts due in unpaid rent and tenant damages to the premises.

When a lease is terminated, the landlord must return the tenant's security deposit within 45 days, including simple interest at the statutory rate. Interest accrues at six-month intervals from the day the tenant gives the security deposit and does not compound.

Security deposits may be withheld by the landlord to cover

- unpaid rent;
- losses due to breach or violation of lease terms (the landlord is entitled only to the actual financial loss—*damages*—caused by the breach); and

- cost of repairs of damage to leased premises in excess of ordinary wear and tear.

Landlords who wish to withhold deposits to cover damages must present to their tenants, within 30 days of the termination of the lease, a statement of damages including a written list of repair costs *actually incurred*. Failure to comply with this could make them liable to the tenant for three times the amount of the security deposit retained, plus reasonable attorneys' fees. The landlords' right to recover from the security deposit any unpaid rent or rental income lost due to breach of lease can also be lost.

An action concerning security deposits may be brought by tenants any time during tenancy or within two years after its termination.

State law requires that every landlord maintain a **records system** showing the dates and amounts of rent paid by tenants and showing that receipts of some form were given to each tenant for each cash rent payment.

MISCELLANEOUS REQUIREMENTS

Note that Baltimore County and City landlords must give tenants of multifamily dwellings notice when they are located in **floodplain areas**, as discussed in Chapter 3 of the principal text.

Owners of residential rental units in Baltimore City must file an **annual registration statement** with the Baltimore City Commissioner of Housing and Community Development, whether the units are occupied or not, and pay a registration fee. Other jurisdictions also may have registration requirements and conduct periodic inspections.

Owners of multifamily residential rental property are required by State law to post in a conspicuous place a sign listing the name, address and telephone number of the property owner or managing agent. The information may instead be included in the lease or the rent receipt.

SALE OF LEASED PREMISES

Unless specified to the contrary in the lease, the purchaser of a property occupied by a tenant under a lease is bound by the conditions and terms of that lease just as the original landlord was. A purchaser not wishing to become a landlord should include a clause in the property purchase contract requiring that the premises be delivered unoccupied and vacant at the time of settlement. Baltimore City law requires a landlord to give the tenant the **right of first refusal** before the leased premises can be conveyed to a third party.

TERMINATION OF TENANCIES IN GENERAL

A lease on Maryland real estate may be terminated by any of the following circumstances:

- Expiration of the term stated in the lease (Note: Although no additional notice to either party is required by common law, Maryland statutes require a 30-day notice.)
- The lessee's purchase or redemption of the fee simple estate from the lessor or the lessee's acquisition of title to that estate superior to that of his lessor
- Mutual agreement between the lessor and lessee
- Destruction of the premises by fire or unavoidable accident except where the property can be restored by ordinary repairs in a few days or within a stipulated period (Note: This termination is effective if the lease is for a term of seven years or less and if the lease did not provide otherwise.)
- Cancellation, as granted by a court of law on the petition of the aggrieved or injured party, when there has been a breach of any covenant or condition of the lease
- Eviction of the tenant as a result of litigation
- In Baltimore City, a tenant's paying 60 days' advance rent to dissolve or terminate any residential lease
- A mortgage on the premises is foreclosed that was entered into prior to entering into the leasehold agreement

Termination of Periodic Tenancies

The requirements to terminate **periodic tenancies** differ throughout the State. In all counties except Montgomery County and Baltimore City, the *landlord must give the tenant written notice* to terminate, as follows:

- One week for a week-to-week tenancy

- One month for a month-to-month tenancy
- Three months for a year-to-year tenancy

By contrast, a *tenant's parol (oral) notice* is sufficient to terminate such tenancies. If landlords can prove that the tenants gave such notice, they do not need to give their own notice to those tenants.

In Montgomery County, the parties may agree in writing to longer or shorter notice periods. The local laws of Baltimore City generally require a landlord to give the following written notice to terminate:

- 60 days for a tenancy of less than one year, at sufferance or *pur autre vie*
- 90 days for a periodic tenancy
- 30 days in all other cases

A tenant may terminate any of these tenancies by giving the landlord 30 days' notice.

When a landlord consents to a **holdover tenant's** remaining on the premises, as described in the text, the holdover tenant becomes a week-to-week tenant if the lease status was week to week prior to the holdover. In all other cases, the tenant becomes a month-to-month tenant unless the lease specifies otherwise and this provision is initialed by the tenant. A tenant under a lease who unlawfully holds over beyond the termination of the lease is liable to the landlord for actual damages that may be caused by the holding over.

Landlords' Rights to Summary Dispossession

Landlords who give the required notice or have court orders for termination of tenancy may dispossess tenants and repossess property by simple court suit before a district court judge. The length of notice landlords must give tenants before beginning **dispossession proceedings** is generally one month in renewable monthly tenancies or in tenancies with a fixed term and no provision for renewal. For automatically renewable yearly tenancies, this notice (with certain exceptions) is three months; for renewable monthly or weekly tenancies, it is one month or one week.

Tenant Refusal to Comply

If the tenant or person in possession refuses to comply with the written request to remove from the property, the landlord may make a complaint in writing to the district court of the county where the property is located. The court issues a summons, which is served by the sheriff to the tenant, to appear before the court, and an attested copy is affixed to the property in a conspicuous place. This is considered sufficient notice.

Failure to Pay Rent

In actions of summary ejectment for failure to pay rent where the landlords are awarded judgments allowing restitution of the leased premises, tenants have the **right of redemption** of the premises. This may be done at any time before the actual execution of an eviction order. Tenants must pay in cash, certified check or money order, all court costs awarded and all back rent due to landlords.

Back Rent on Renewal of Lease

Tenants or assignees who apply to their landlords for renewal under a covenant in their leases giving them the right to renew must produce vouchers or evidence showing payment of rent accrued for three years preceding this demand and application. If tenants do not provide such proof, landlords, before executing the renewal of the lease, are entitled to demand and recover not more than three years' back rent, in addition to any renewal fine that may be provided for in the lease. This commonly occurs in situations involving ground rent.

If there is no demand or payment of rent for more than 20 consecutive years, landlords not only lose the rental but also the reversion of the property. Landlords under any legal disability when the 20-year period expires have two years after the removal of the disability to assert their rights. Landlords' failure to demand rent for 20 years could result in the tenants' receiving fee simple title.

Receipts for Tenants' Rental

In Anne Arundel County, unless the tenant makes payment by check or rents the property for commercial or business purposes, the landlord is required to give the tenant a receipt showing the amount of payment and the time it covers. On conviction of violating this section of the law, any person or agent forfeits the rent for the period in question.

In other counties, when the tenant makes payment other than by check, the landlord or the landlord's agent must give the tenant a receipt.

Surrender of Premises

When a lease contains a covenant or promise by the tenant to leave, restore, surrender or yield the leased premises in good repair, this does not bind the tenant to erect any similar building or pay for any building destroyed by fire or otherwise if the damage was not due to the negligence or fault of the tenant.

Landlords may ask the district court to seize and sell tenants' personal property for unpaid rent by filing a petition. Landlords may do this only if tenancy has continued for longer than three months (by written lease or periodic tenancy) or was *at will*. Both the landlords' right to and the court's taking of tenants' property are called *distraint*.

A rental agreement must clearly state such information as when tenancy expires, when rent accrues or whether rent is to be paid in advance or in arrears. If it does not, a court may find the agreement's terms too vague, and deny the landlord's request for distraint.

PROHIBITED RESIDENTIAL LEASE PROVISIONS

In Maryland, the following provisions are prohibited in residential leases:

- A provision (**cognovit clause**) whereby tenants authorize another person to **confess judgment** on a claim arising from the lease.

- A provision under which the tenant agrees to waive or forgo any rights or remedies against the landlord as provided by law.
- A provision allowing the landlord to charge a penalty for late payment of rent more than 5 percent of the amount of rent due for the period in which the rent is delinquent. For weekly rentals, this late charge may not exceed $3 per week, nor may such charges exceed $12 per month.
- Any provision under which the tenant waives his or her right to a jury trial.
- Any provision under which the tenant agrees to a period for the landlord's **notice to quit** (in the event that the tenant breaches the lease terms) that is less than the period prescribed by law. Both parties, however, are free to agree to a period that is longer than is prescribed by law.
- Any provision authorizing the landlord to take possession of the leased premises or any of the tenant's personal property unless the lease has been terminated by operation of law and such personal property has been abandoned by the tenant.
- Any provision (**exculpatory clause**) intended to exempt or hold the landlord harmless from liability to the tenant or any other person for any injury, loss, damage or liability arising from the landlord's omission, fault, negligence or other misconduct on or about the leased premises in areas that are not under the tenant's control. This includes stairways, elevators, hallways and so forth. This type of provision is contrary to public policy and void.
- A provision allowing the automatic renewal of the lease term. Any such provision not signed or initialed by the tenant is unenforceable.
- A requirement that the tenant give the landlord a longer period of notice to terminate the tenancy than the period granted the landlord to similarly notify the tenant.

All of the preceding provisions, if inserted into a Maryland lease, are considered **unenforceable**.

WITHHOLDING RENT

State law requires that a landlord provide and maintain premises for tenants that are free of defects and do not present substantial and serious threat of danger to the life, health and safety of the tenants. Where **hazardous conditions** exist on leased property, a tenant may give the landlord written notice by certified mail of the conditions and wait a period of 30 days. If the hazardous conditions are not corrected, a tenant can withhold rent from the landlord or pay it into an escrow account for necessary repairs. Such conditions include fire or health hazards or other defects that may threaten the safety or occupancy of renters, such as

- lack of adequate sewage disposal facilities,

- infestation of rodents in two or more dwelling units and
- the existence of lead-based paint on surfaces within the unit.

The Baltimore City Code holds that there is an implied **warranty of habitability** by a landlord that the premises are fit for human habitation. It also provides for remedies for tenants if the premises are unsafe and dirty to the extent that tenants' health is threatened. The warranty of habitability differs from **rent escrow laws** in that tenants have the use of their rent money to make those repairs the landlord has failed to complete. Under the rent escrow, rent must be paid into an account where it is held until the repairs are made.

The district court can order tenants to pay rents into an **rent escrow account** of the court or administrative agency of the county. If the tenant fails to pay rent accrued or as it becomes due, the court, upon certification of the account, can give judgment in favor of the landlord and issue a warrant for possession. Upon final disposition of the action, the rent escrow account is distributed in accordance with the judgment or hearing.

Note that minor, not dangerous, defects or housing code violations that go uncorrected are not considered just cause for nonpayment of rent.

HOUSING DISCRIMINATION AGAINST ELDERLY

A landlord, real estate broker or real estate agent is prohibited from refusing to rent or sell a house to persons 62 years of age or older solely based on their age.

LEASE AGREEMENT FORMS

A number of lease forms are available from local realty boards or associations, property owner associations and tenant organizations. Any landlord who offers more than four dwelling units for rent on one parcel of property or at one location and who rents by means of written leases substantially increases the requirements concerning the form of written lease.

RETALIATORY EVICTIONS

A landlord may not evict tenants, increase rent or decrease any services to which they are entitled for their doing any of the following things:

- Filing written complaints with the landlord or with a public agency against the landlord
- Filing a lawsuit against the landlord
- Joining a tenants' organization

SAFETY REQUIREMENTS

Smoke detectors must be installed in all multifamily buildings and hotels constructed before 1975 and having four to nine units and in all buildings with more than nine units. The landlord is responsible for the installation, repair or replacement of the detectors. The occupant of a one-family, two-family or three-family residential dwelling constructed before July 1975 is required to equip the apartment with at least one approved smoke detector and to maintain it.

A smoke detector operated both by battery and by alternating current (AC) must be installed in every newly constructed residential dwelling unit. At least one smoke detector must be installed on each level, including a basement but excluding an attic.

Sprinkler systems must be installed in every newly constructed dormitory, hotel, lodging or rooming house, town house and multifamily residential dwelling. Sprinkler systems are not required if a dwelling unit is not serviced by a public water supply system.

LEASE OPTION AGREEMENTS

A **lease option** agreement includes any lease that contains a clause giving the tenant the option to purchase the land-lord's interest in the property until some specified date. No lease option on improved residential property in Mary-land, with or without a ground rent interest, is valid unless it contains the statement "THIS IS NOT A CONTRACT TO BUY" in capital letters. It must also contain a clear statement of the option's

purpose and effect with respect to the ultimate purchase of the property.

SOURCES OF ASSISTANCE

Baltimore Neighborhoods, Inc., a private nonprofit civil rights agency working in behalf of fair housing and tenants' rights in the Baltimore area, publishes guides to laws covering tenant/landlord relations in Baltimore City, the counties and the State. These guides, revised annually to incorporate new laws, may be purchased from the organization at 2217 St. Paul St., Baltimore, MD 21218.

MOBILE HOME PARKS

Title 8A of the *Real Property Article* sets forth the rights and responsibilities of mobile home tenants and owners. It addresses such matters as park rules, maintenance and tenancy. Although the particulars of this law are too detailed for this volume, a licensee planning to own or manage a mobile home park should become familiar with the law's provisions.

QUESTIONS

1. Sampson sold a house he owned that was occupied by Rawlins under a one-year lease having six months to run. Therefore

   a. Rawlins must vacate at the closing of the sale.
   b. Rawlins's lease continues until its expiration.
   c. the lease terminates at closing.
   d. the lease is not binding on the new owner.

2. A landlord holding a tenant's security deposit of $500 is required to

   a. credit the deposit account $20 interest per year.
   b. allow the tenant 5 percent simple interest per year.
   c. return the deposit within 30 days after termination of the lease.
   d. give the tenant a receipt or be liable to the tenant for a sum of $250.

3. Which of the following leases need NOT be in writing, acknowledged and recorded in Maryland?

   a. Seven-year apartment lease
   b. Eight-year residential lease
   c. Nine-year commercial lease
   d. Ten-year residential lease

4. John Builder has just completed a new house, which he is offering for sale at $68,000 with fee simple title. If, to satisfy an immediate buyer, he creates a ground lease requiring $240 a year ground rent at an 8 percent redemption rate, then

   a. the property may not be redeemed for at least 50 years.
   b. he can reduce the price to $65,000.
   c. he can reduce the price to $56,000.
   d. the in-fee price would be $71,000.

5. Arthur Buyer is interested in buying a residence for $40,000 with a ground rent of $180. Arthur will receive

   a. a deed conveying to him a fee simple interest.
   b. an assignment conveying to him a leasehold estate subject to an annual ground rent of $180.
   c. no deed until such time as he redeems the ground rent.
   d. a fee simple deed after paying ground rent for five years.

6. A man who owns and occupies his home and pays a semiannual ground rent owns an estate in real estate that is called a(n)

   a. fee simple estate.
   b. leasehold estate.
   c. estate at will.
   d. estate at sufferance.

7. Ground rents are sometimes originated to

   a. reduce the amount of cash required to purchase a property.
   b. force the tenant to keep the property in good repair.
   c. provide further assurances to the mortgagee.
   d. prevent the lender from foreclosing.

8. The ground rent on a residence is $180 a year, and the lease has been in effect for more than five years. A redemption at

   a. 5 percent will require $3,200.
   b. 6 percent will require $3,000.
   c. 10 percent will require $6,400.
   d. 12 percent will require $6,000.

9. The right of a landlord to have a court seize and sell a tenant's personal property for unpaid rent is called

   a. ejectment.
   b. abandonment.
   c. dispossession.
   d. distraint.

10. Which of the following provisions, if included in residential leases in Maryland, is enforceable?

   a. Tenants agree to pay the landlord a 5 percent penalty for late rent payments
   b. Tenants agree to let landlords use their passkeys to take possession of tenants' property if tenants fall more than one month behind in rent payments
   c. Tenants agree to waive or forgo any rights or remedies against landlords provided by law
   d. Tenants waive their rights to jury trial

20
Fair Housing

OVERVIEW

Competent real estate licensees realize that fair housing compliance is very demanding. It requires knowledge of applicable federal, state and local laws, each of which often has it own list of protected groups and of prohibited and required activities.

In this chapter, the term *Commission* refers to the State of Maryland Commission on Human Relations.

FEDERAL FAIR HOUSING LAWS

Since Maryland has laws and enforcement mechanisms "substantially equivalent" to the federal laws, no action under the Federal Fair Housing Law of 1968 and its amendments may be undertaken. The Maryland avenues must be followed.

A person aggrieved in the area of racial discrimination on any property—real, personal, residential, commercial or industrial—may seek relief under the Civil Rights Act of 1866, in Federal Court.

The Maryland law has exceptions that parallel those in the 1968 Fair Housing act.

The Commission is required to make a written report of the findings of any investigation of a real estate licensee to the Real Estate Commission for appropriate action.

Counties, municipalities and other local governments are also empowered to enact ordinances and extend protection to additional groups.

DISCRIMINATION IN HOUSING

The Maryland law on fair housing is administered by the State of Maryland Commission on Human Relations and enforced by the appropriate State court.

There are many examples in this statute of unlawful discriminatory housing practices against persons because of their race, color, religion, sex, handicap, marital status, familial status or national origin:

- Refusing to sell, rent, or negotiate after a bona fide offer

- Making unavailable or denying a dwelling, or representing that a property is not available for inspection, sale or rent when it is in fact available
- Discriminating in terms, conditions, privileges of sale or rental of a dwelling
- Discriminating in the provision of related service or facilities
- Making or ordering to be made any publication, notice or statement concerning properties for sale or rent indicating any preference, limitation or discrimination
- Seeking, for profit, to induce any person to sell or rent a dwelling by making representations regarding the entry of a protected group into an area

Special Provisions for Handicapped Persons

In addition to protections for the handicapped as mentioned in the previous list, these details are added on their behalf:

- Discrimination against a handicapped applicant or a non-handicapped applicant who will have a handicapped person residing in the dwelling after it is sold, rented or made available
- Discrimination in sale, rental or availability of a property
- Discrimination in terms, conditions or privileges of sale or rental or in connection with the dwelling after sale or rental
- Refusal to permit reasonable modifications of existing premises occupied or to be occupied by

handicapped individuals (These modifications are those necessary to give the handicapped person full enjoyment of the dwelling and are made at tenants' expense and with the tenants' agreement to restore the premises to their condition before the modification.)
- Refusal to make reasonable accommodations in rules, policies, practices or services when such accommodations are necessary to give handicapped persons equal opportunity to use and enjoy a dwelling
- Failure to design or construct a multifamily dwelling for first occupancy so that the public use and common areas are readily accessible to and usable by handicapped persons, all doors for passage into and within all premises within the dwelling are wide enough to accommodate wheelchairs, and all premises have suitable adaptive design features (for example, an accessible route into and through the dwelling; light switches, electrical outlets, thermostats and other environmental controls in accessible locations; reinforcements in bathroom walls to allow later installation of grab bars; and kitchens and bathrooms designed so that individuals in wheelchairs can maneuver about the space.)

Real Estate Industry Groups

The law forbids any person or business entity that engages in real estate related transactions

- to discriminate against any person in making available a transaction or in the terms or conditions of a transaction because of membership in a protected group or
- to deny access to or membership or participation in a multiple-listing service, brokers' organization or other service, organization or facility relating to the business of selling or renting dwellings, or to discriminate in the terms or conditions of membership or participation based on protected group status.

Threats, Coercion, Intimidation, Etc., Against Persons Seeking Housing and Against Others Who Encourage Them

The statute makes it unlawful to coerce, intimidate, threaten, interfere with or retaliate against persons who seek to exercise the rights granted by this law or persons who encourage others to exercise such rights. Persons guilty of such actions may be fined not more than $1,000, or suffer imprisonment for not more than one year or both. If the violation results in bodily injury, $10,000 and ten years. If in death, imprisonment for any term of years or for life.

The Complaint Process

Complaints to the Commission must be filed not more than one year after the violation by the aggrieved person or by the Commission on its own initiative. The complaint must be in writing and made under oath. The Commission has ten days to notify respondents (the ones complained about). Respondents' answers to complaints must be filed within 10 days of receipt of notice and must also be made under oath.

The Commission seeks to reconcile the parties and get them to enter into a settlement agreement or to agree to arbitration. Agreements are made public unless the parties agree otherwise or the Commission decides no public purpose would be served.

The Commission may sue to enforce an agreement that a respondent has breached.

At the time a complaint is first received, the Commission may also authorize a civil action in circuit court of the county where the property is located for relief of the complaining party. Having done this, the Commission may still proceed with its administrative proceedings.

If an aggrieved party initiates a civil action under Federal or State law seeking relief for a discriminatory housing practice, the Commission may review the complaint and refer the matter to the State Attorney General, but may not continue further on the same charges.

Anyone who deliberately submits false information to the Commission as it investigates or who fails to make full disclosure or who changes previous records, reports or accounts can be punished by a fine of not more than $100,000, imprisonment of not more than one year or both.

Aggrieved persons may begin civil actions in an appropriate State court not later than two years after the discriminatory action. They may file no such civil actions, based on the same discrimination, after the Commission or a State or local agency has succeeded in producing a conciliation agreement that the aggrieved parties agreed to, except to enforce such agreement.

Relief granted in a civil action may not set aside any lease or sales contract to other bona fide purchasers or tenants who did not have actual notice of the filing of a complaint with the Commission or of the civil action.

Pattern of Discrimination

When the Commission believes there is a pattern of discrimination or resistance to the rights granted by this law, it may commence a civil action in circuit court. The court may award preventive relief or grant temporary or permanent injunctions and restraining orders against those responsible for violations. It may also award, in addition to attorney's fees, monetary damages to aggrieved persons in amounts not to exceed $50,000 for a first violation and $100,000 for subsequent violations.

COMMERCIAL PROPERTY

Neither the owners or the operators of commercial property, their agents and employees, nor any persons licensed or regulated by the State may discriminate against an individual in the terms, conditions or privileges of property leased for commercial usage, or in the provision of services or facilities in connection with the property, because of the individual's

race, color, religion, sex, age [*sic.*], handicap, marital status or national origin.

THE REAL ESTATE BROKERS ACT

The Brokers Act also addresses discrimination against protected groups.

Whether or not acting for monetary gain, a person may not knowingly induce or attempt to induce another person to sell or rent a dwelling or otherwise transfer real estate or knowingly discourage or attempt to discourage another person from purchasing real estate

- by making representations regarding the entry or prospective entry into a neighborhood of individuals of a particular race, color, sex, religion or national origin;
- by making representations regarding the existing or potential proximity of real property owned or used by individuals of a particular race, color, sex, religion or national origin; or
- by representing that the existing or potential proximity of real property owned or used by individuals of a particular race, color, sex, religion or national origin will or may result in the lowering of property values; a change in the racial, religious or ethnic character of the block, neighborhood or area; an increase in criminal or antisocial behavior in the area; or a decline in the quality of schools serving the area.

A person may not provide **financial assistance** by loan, gift or otherwise to another person if the person has actual knowledge that the financial assistance will be used in a transaction that results from a violation of these prohibitions.

Solicitation of Residential Listings

If one of the purposes of the solicitation or attempted solicitation is to change the racial composition of a neighborhood, a person may not solicit or attempt to solicit the listing of residential properties for sale or lease by in-person door-to-door solicitation, telephone solicitation or mass distribution of circulars.

The Maryland Broker's Act empowers the Real Estate Commission to identify and designate certain localities as conservation areas. In these areas and for limited time periods, all advertising of properties for sale and the use of "For Sale" signs is suspended. Brokerage firms may not solicit listings from owners of such properties, but may list them when approached by their owners. Requirements for establishing such areas is presently so cumbersome that not one such area has been identified for more than a decade.

State Enforcement

Fair housing provisions of the Brokers Act and COMAR are enforced by the State Real Estate Commission. Fair housing violations forbidden by the Brokers Act are prosecuted by the Maryland Attorney General. Courts finding licensees guilty of such charges are required to report their decisions to the Commission.

Local Laws and Their Enforcement

Chartered counties are empowered to enforce fair housing law violations with fines or penalties not to exceed those provided in the federal Fair Housing Act Amendments of 1988 and 1993.

Baltimore City law prohibits the solicitation of residential properties for purchase or sale by general door-to-door solicitations, in person or by telephone, or by the mass distribution of circulars. There are no exceptions to the law. Solicitations as a result of personal referrals, general knowledge that a property is for sale or offerings by an owner also constitute violations of the law. The court has added that any uninvited call or visit could constitute a violation of this ordinance.

Laws concerning solicitation vary from jurisdiction to jurisdiction. It is the responsibility of licensees to be familiar with the local laws.

Baltimore County law provides several methods of **canvassing** that are not considered solicitation. They include advertisements in bona fide newspapers of general circulation, radio or television; literature distributed through the U.S. mail; legitimate personal referrals; contacts with property owners resulting from the owners' having personally advertised the property for sale; and solicitation for the purpose of obtaining information for appraisals or similar collection of general sales or market data.

Violation of either the Baltimore City or Baltimore County law is punishable as a misdemeanor, with **penalties**, upon conviction, of a fine, imprisonment or both.

EDUCATIONAL REQUIREMENTS

The Real Estate Commission enforces fair housing practices. Commission General Regulations 11, 14 and 17 require that all license applicants be instructed in the human relations aspects of the practice of real estate, including study of fair housing laws and the effects of such undesirable practices as exploitation, steering, block-busting, prejudicial solicitation, discriminatory practices, misleading advertising and related activities. This instruction is mandated in the pre-license education requirements for salesperson and for broker.

DISCRIMINATION IN FINANCING

It is unlawful for any bank, savings and loan institution, credit union, insurance company or other creditor to deny a housing loan or credit to persons who apply or to discriminate against them in the fixing of the down payment, interest rate, duration or other terms or conditions of such a loan because of the race, color, religion, creed, marital status, familial status, sex, national origin or physical or mental handicap of such person or of any member, stockholder, director, officer or employee of such person or of the prospective occupants, lessees or tenants of the dwelling for which the loan application is made.

HUD FAIR HOUSING ADVERTISING GUIDELINES

Brokers are urged to obtain the current version of **Fair Housing Advertising Guidelines** from the Department of Housing and Urban Development.

MARYLAND HUMAN RELATIONS LAW

Article 49B of the Annotated Code of Maryland prohibits many forms of discrimination against various lists of protected groups. It addresses business firms licensed by the State and is wide in its scope.

It is unlawful for any firm licensed by the Department of Labor, Licensing, and Regulation or for any person affiliated with such a firm ". . . to refuse, withhold from, deny . . . any person accommodations, advantages, facilities, privileges, sales, or services because of the race, sex, creed, color, national origin, marital status [*sic.*], or physical or mental handicap of any person."

The Commission may find that a complaint is without merit and there is no probable cause to proceed against the respondent. Complainants in such cases may request reconsideration of their complaints. If the Commission denies a request for reconsideration of a finding of *no probable cause*, the denial is a final order appealable to the circuit court unless the U.S. Equal Employment Opportunity Commission has jurisdiction over the subject matter of the complaint.

If the Human Relations Commission, after proper investigation and hearing, concludes that a **respondent**—the person against whom the charge was brought—has engaged in any of the unlawful practices listed above, it may seek an order assessing a civil penalty against the respondent not exceeding $500 for a first offense. If it is the second offense within five years, the penalty can be in an amount not more than $1,000. If there were two prior offenses within the last seven years, the maximum penalty would be $2,500. If the respondent is a natural person—an individual rather than a firm or organization—the penalty may be imposed without regard to the time periods between previous violations.

QUESTIONS

1. James and Frances Miller, who are African American, tell the real estate salesperson that they need a three-bedroom house in the $120,000 to $130,000 price range that is within walking distance of an elementary school. The salesperson, after identifying the Millers as genuine prospects, finds a house on Judson Street that meets all the Millers' requirements, but the salesperson knows that the residents of the neighborhood are unhappy about African Americans moving into the area. The agent should

   a. refrain from telling the Millers about this particular house.
   b. tell them about the house, but suggest that they would be happier in another neighborhood.
   c. file a complaint with the Human Relations Commission.
   d. inform the Millers about the availability of the house and arrange to show them the listing.

2. With respect to fair housing, all persons engaged in real estate transactions

   a. must be familiar with all applicable federal, state and local anti-discrimination statutes and ordinances.
   b. carry E&O insurance to be protected.
   c. may refuse to be held liable.
   d. have the right to decide what is best for their customers and clients.

3. Two salespersons are working on a residential listing in a neighborhood that was formerly all white. They

   a. are proper in not showing this listing to white prospects.
   b. violate state and federal laws when they determine whether or not to show a listing based on a prospect's race.
   c. need not introduce into the neighborhood anyone not of the predominant race of the neighborhood.
   d. should have a salesperson of the same race as the prospect show the property.

4. A broker approaches homeowners seeking to list their property for sale. They had not been thinking of selling, but the broker tells them, "The time to sell is now," because the neighborhood is experiencing a large minority group influx and that the value of their property, ". . . is sure to drop," if they wait any longer. This broker's behavior illustrates

   a. blockbusting.
   b. steering.
   c. blind advertising.
   d. redlining.

21
Environmental Issues and the Real Estate Transaction

OVERVIEW

The State of Maryland, like most states, faces complex environmental challenges. Almost all of them call for balancing economic growth with human safety and quality of life. These tensions can pit the rights of property owners against the wishes of others for preservation or restoration of natural resources. Literally hundreds of statutes, ordinances, and regulations are written statewide each year to address these matters.

MULTIPLE CHALLENGES

Some of the greatest areas of concern are loss of woodlands, farmlands, and tidal- and nontidal wetlands. These overlap such ecological issues as endangered species, clean air and clean water, fisheries and other wild life. Recreation and camping space needs are also part of the puzzle.

A variety of hazards to human health are created by auto emissions and other air and/or water pollution, for example, by ozone, asbestos, radon, radium, lead based paint, wastewater sewerage, indus-

trial waste, leakage from underground storage tanks and acid rain.

Additional areas of concern are stormwater and nutrient runoff management, postmining reclamation activities, water pollution near wellheads and the effects on wildlife and endangered species of dredging and filling of waterways. An ever-increasing problem is disposal of solid waste (garbage and trash) and sludge from water treatment plants and industrial activities.

MEETING THE CHALLENGES

One of the current attempts to balance the conflicting demands of conservation and development is the Governor's *Smart Growth Initiative,* which is designed to motivate local jurisdictions in the State to plan more effectively for growth without sprawl—the wasteful use of space. The State will provide technical guidance for decisions made in such planning and offer motivations for participation.

The Smart Growth Initiative is intended to guide growth wisely. It is not a no-growth plan. Even its name is crafted to attract the participation of such diverse parties as environmentalists and developers. Planning for "smart growth" will include all stakeholders—representatives of every side of the issue—in hopes of getting better cooperation from all parties in carrying out the decisions made.

A Multilevel Approach

The State reaches upward, outward and inward in its efforts: upward toward federal agencies, outward toward neighboring states and inward to subdivisions and municipalities.

To this last group the State typically grants enabling powers to authorize their participation through zoning and other environmentally related activities. The various subdivisions are authorized to set standards even more rigorous than those set by the State. They may not, however, be less strict.

Cooperative Approaches

It is rare that an environmental issue can be handled effectively by the Maryland State Government acting alone. Its activities and interests overlap and interact with those of the federal government, neighboring states, Maryland subdivisions and municipalities, and private and corporate citizens.

ENFORCEMENT

Enforcement of standards, set forth in statutes, regulations and ordinances, is carried out by the Maryland Department of the Environment (MDE) except in cases where county enforcement capabilities and resources are comparable to those of the Department. The Secretary of MDE may delegate enforcement powers to such counties for a two-year period.

REGIONAL COMPACTS

Over the years, the State has entered into agreements with neighboring states. Its 1987 compact with New York and Pennsylvania is designed to protect groundwater in the Susquehanna River Basin until 2087. Such *compacts* take as long as a decade to negotiate and confirm.

Another interstate arrangement was made in response to the Federal Water Pollution Control Act of 1972. By 1993, Maryland, Pennsylvania, Virginia, the District of Columbia and the federal government (EPA) signed the Chesapeake Bay Agreement. This compact was amended, enlarged and strengthened in 1985, 1987, 1992, 1993 and 1994. Further enhancements concerning pollution of the tributaries feeding into the Bay are now the subject of study.

In addition to approval by the State subdivisions affected, the Corps of Engineers must coordinate with other federal agencies its activities in granting permits for wetland fill. These include the Environmental Protection Agency, the U.S. Department of Agriculture, the Fish and Wildlife Service, the National Oceanic and Atmospheric Administration, the Federal Advisory Council on Historic Preservation and certain state preservation officers, and the National Marine Fisheries Service.

Such agreements are statutory. They require cooperation among and within the states and their subdivisions and with the U.S. Army Corps of Engineers. Other agreements and programs are voluntary. Recent programs are "inspirational" in nature—designed to focus attention on common problems and opportunities and to inspire action.

FILLING OF WETLANDS RESISTED

Filling wetlands, for whatever purpose, is regarded as one of the most environmentally pernicious of actions. It may be permitted only when no alternative course of action is available or when new areas of wetland to compensate for those being filled will be created by the person seeking a permit. The replacement area ratios range from one-new-for-each-one-lost to 4.5-new-for-each-one-lost.

When enforced by overlapping bureaucracies, the rules have sometimes proved extremely complex for those who apply for approvals, especially for filling operations. For instance, there have even been as many as three different definitions of the term *wetlands* in force at one time.

IMPACT ON RESIDENTIAL REAL ESTATE

Many of these environmental issues directly and indirectly affect availability of residential housing. As a consequence of their efforts to preserve agricultural space and wetlands, various levels of government reduce the amount of land available for development. For instance, the pres-

ent policy of Maryland is not just to maintain but to increase the present quantity of wetlands.

The State is paying down the Outdoor Recreation Land Loan of 1989 and purchasing more land with part of the State Transfer Tax imposed on most residential real estate transactions. The tax also is applied toward the Agricultural Land Preservation Fund, the Rural Legacy Program, the Heritage Conservation Fund and the operation of Program Open Space.

In seeking to achieve environmental and public safety goals, the State and its subdivisions impose regulatory and impact fees and increasingly require costly safety measures and techniques protective of both persons and the environment.

By slowing development and imposing fees upon developers, which are passed along to consumers, and by using settlements as a revenue source, governments make it more costly for people to buy homes.

ENVIRONMENTAL LEGISLATION AND REGULATION

Licensees should become aware of the numerous federal, state and local environmental land use regulations and agencies and how they affect development. The *Environment* and *Natural Resources* Articles of the Annotated Code of Maryland contain statutes governing waters of the state, soil and forest conservation and sanitary facilities. Related regulations are made by the MDE.

In addition, State and federal legislation concerning lead levels in certain rental properties place substantial responsibilities and burdens on investor-owners of many income properties and their agents. At the same time, these laws allow investors to limit their liability for lead poisoning by following certain procedures. A more complete discussion of this program appears toward the end of this chapter.

Owners of certain underground storage tanks containing petroleum products must remove or pay for the removal of tanks that leak. MDE regulations set standards for evidence of financial responsibility of owners for costs of cleanup, corrective action and liability.

MARYLAND DEPARTMENT OF THE ENVIRONMENT

The MDE provides basic information about **radon** on its web site: http://www.mde.state.md.us/reference/factsheets/radon.html

It points out the presence of household radon in Maryland and cites the danger of continued exposure to it:

> Some Maryland homes have radon levels higher than 200 pico-curies per liter (pCi/l) of air (pico-curies per liter is a measure of radiation). These levels are 50 times higher than the action guidelines set by the U.S. Environmental Protection Agency. By spending your lifetime in a house with radon levels of 10 pCi/l you have a lung cancer risk similar to smoking nearly a pack of cigarettes a day.

The web site suggests that persons with inquiries about radon contact the EPA (federal) Hotline: 1-800-767-7236.

The MDE is testing for **radium**—a naturally occurring radioactive metal—in wells in portions of Anne Arundel, Baltimore, Cecil, Harford, Kent, Queen Anne's and Prince George's Counties. It projects the danger from drinking water with radium in it thus:

> (The) Environmental Protection Agency (EPA) estimates that there may be some long-term health risk from drinking water containing radium above EPA standards. According to EPA, if 10,000 people were to consume two liters of this water every day for 50 years, there might be one additional fatal cancer among the 10,000 exposed individuals. Consuming water at this level is comparable to receiving one routine chest x-ray per year, with the exposure increasing as the concentrations increase.

Air and Radiation Management Administration

Within the MDE, the Air and Radiation Management Administration, among its other duties, sets and enforces standards for **asbestos** removal and encapsulation projects and licenses people who work in that field.

Waste Management Administration

Also within the MDE is the Waste Management Administration which deals with environmental restoration and land redevelopment, oil control, **lead poisoning, solid waste, scrap tires, sewage sludge** and **hazardous materials**. It oversees above-ground storage tanks for oil and gas and underground tanks for storage of regulated substances. It seeks to identify, prioritize and abate contaminated sites.

Water Management Administration

Among the most important functions within the MDE are those given to the Water Management Administration, which seeks to protect **drinking water**. With its 62 inspectors, it also oversees tidal and nontidal wetland, floodplains, water appropriations, waterway and floodplain construction, sediment control, stormwater management, coal mining and oil and gas exploration.

LEAD PAINT POISONING REDUCTION ACT

The purpose of this law is " . . . to reduce the incidence of childhood lead poisoning, while maintaining the stock of available affordable rental housing." This act, the environmental law that affects more existing residential properties than any other, undergirds Maryland's Lead Paint Poisoning Prevention Program.

There is broad-based scientific agreement that exposure to lead-based paint can produce devastating results in children and newborns. This law is a serious attempt to reduce the exposure of children under six and of pregnant women to the effects of lead-based paint in residential rental properties built before 1979.

Children and Mothers Targeted

The program makes children under six and pregnant women with EBL (Elevated

Blood Lead) levels eligible for specific financial relief for medical treatment ($7,500) and moving to lead-safe housing ($9,500). These amounts come either from landlords or their insurance companies. Investors wishing to limit their liability to their tenants for lead poisoning must bring their property into compliance with "lead-free" or "lead-safe" standards and keep it that way.

Plan Encourages Modest Settlements

The plan doesn't actually limit or "cap" the liability of landlords. Rather, it makes them eligible to present "qualified offers" to their tenants with EBL levels of up to $7,500 for medical expenses and up to $9,500 for relocation and rent supplement expenses. If tenants with elevated levels of lead in their blood accept the "qualified offer," they give up the right to sue the landlord for larger sums. They get their money as soon as needed and don't have to face the prolonged uncertainty of initiating a lawsuit that is particularly difficult to win.

Companies insuring properties that are or have been made lead free or lead safe are required to provide liability coverage for lead paint poisoning up to $17,000—the total of $7,500 and $9,500.

Scope of Program to Increase

The requirements on landlords increase periodically.

- On and after February 24, 2001, owners of affected properties shall ensure that at least 50% of their affected properties have satisfied the risk reduction standard specified in this subtitle, without regard to the number of affected properties in which there has been a change in occupancy.

- On and after February 24, 2006, owners of affected properties shall ensure that 100% of their affected properties in which a person at risk resides, and of whom the owner has been notified in writing, have satisfied the *risk reduction standard*.

- On and after February 24, 2006, an owner of affected properties shall ensure that 100% of the owner's affected properties in which a person at risk does *not* reside have satisfied the *modified* risk reduction standard.

Properties to Be Registered

Under this law, effective since October 1994, more than 50,000 rental dwelling properties have already been registered with the MDE. Owners must register every residential dwelling unit built before 1950 and pay an annual fee of $10. Owners of properties built between 1950 and 1978 who choose not to participate must pay a fee of $5 per unit per year. Those participating pay $10 per unit per year. All registrations must be renewed annually. Owners of properties built after 1979 are allowed to join the program and submit to its requirements.

Licensees' Responsibilities

Licensees representing landlords who have affected residential rental properties share their legal responsibilities as their agents under this law. They must become conversant with the details of inspection, lead reduction procedures, property registration, periodic renewal of registration, insurance and limitation of liability with respect to lead paint issues.

For this purpose many are taking specialized management courses offered by such groups as the Institute for Real Estate Management (IREM) and Business Owners and Managers Association (BOMA) that focus on this law. In short: education and training are a way of life for licensees who are dedicated to meeting their fiduciary responsibilities.

FEDERAL LAW ALSO APPLIES

The requirements of Maryland law are in addition to and do not take the place of the requirements set forth in federal law concerning lead in residential properties built prior to 1978.

Closing the Real Estate Transaction

OVERVIEW

Whether it is called **settlement**, **closing**, **going to escrow** or some other name, this event is the culmination of real estate brokerage activities. At this meeting title to property passes from sellers to purchasers and then, usually, to the lender. As a result of the closing meeting, purchasers take on long-term debt and sellers get equity funds from sale of their property. From these funds sellers typically pay commissions to their listing broker and satisfy outstanding mortgages or other liens against the property sold. Listing brokers may divide their commissions with in-house affiliates who **assisted** purchasers, intra-company agents who **represented** buyers and sellers, or cooperating brokers who either assisted or represented purchasers.

EVIDENCE OF TITLE

In Maryland, it is customary for buyers to authorize a **title search** and a **binder** (interim commitment) for **mortgagee title insurance** at the time of entering into a purchase contract. In most cases, the settlement officers or attorneys for the lending institution actually order the preparation of an **abstract of title** from the public records. From this abstract they prepare an opinion of the **marketability of the title**. Some attorneys will issue their own **certificates of title**. Alternatively, an abstract may be used by a title company attorney as the basis for offering title insurance.

Lenders typically require mortgagee (lender) title insurance for the protection of their position. State law requires that purchasers be offered **homeowner** (buyer) **title insurance** at every residential closing. Buyers who decline homeowner title insurance are asked to do so in writing.

SETTLEMENTS

Most purchase contracts and sale agreements are closed in the office of a title insurance company, the buyer's attorney, the mortgage lender or the real estate broker. Closing in Maryland is usually performed at a meeting involving buyers, sellers, agents and a settlement officer. **Closing in escrow** is generally not practiced in Maryland.

CLOSING AND TAX STATEMENTS

The buyers' or sellers' attorney or a settlement company officer will prepare the necessary closing statement. Licensees should know how these statements are calculated in order to estimate accurately sellers' expenses of sale and net proceeds from the transaction. They should also be able to estimate for purchasers the amount of additional cash needed at closing to complete the purchase. Most multiple listing service (MLS) systems have an interactive program to help licensees accurately estimate, at an early stage in the sales transaction, expenses and proceeds for both parties. Closing costs are apportioned according to statute, where applicable, and/or by contractual agreement.

Real estate brokers or their salespersons normally are present at settlement, although the interaction is—and should be—principally among any attorneys present representing the parties and the mortgage lender, the officer conducting settlement and the parties to the agreement. Licensees are present for whatever nonlegal services they may be asked to render and, of course, to receive the commission.

By federal law, all owner/sellers must provide the closing agent with their forwarding addresses and Social Security numbers. Corporate sellers must provide their corporate tax identification numbers. All persons must sign an affidavit as to the accuracy of information they have given that will be reported to the IRS. Licensees should make sure that their sellers are prepared to provide all the required information at time of settlement. The closing agent or title company can answer any questions that may arise. This reporting is not required for settlements of mortgage and deed of trust loans when refinancing a property.

EVIDENCE OF RECORDED RELEASE OF MORTGAGE

Persons responsible for disbursement of funds in connection with a settlement at which a transfer of title occurs must mail or deliver to the sellers, within 30 days, evidence of recorded release of mortgage. If the recording of release is delayed beyond the 30-day period for causes beyond their control, they must mail or deliver to the sellers a letter explaining the delay. They must send another letter for each additional delay of 30 days. Failure to follow these rules may subject them to audit of their accounts by the court.

If persons conducting closing properly disburse all funds entrusted to them in the closing procedure within five days, no such evidence is required unless specifically requested by purchasers or vendors.

Vendors and purchasers are to be informed in writing of these requirements before the deed is delivered at the time of settlement.

Part III
The Real Estate License Examination

OVERVIEW

Passing the required state examination is a major challenge for persons seeking real estate licenses. Every applicant would like to pass the exam on the first try, not only to speed up the licensing process but also to reduce cost, minimize inconvenience and avoid embarrassment.

During the first year the current examination was used in Maryland, approximately 22 percent of test takers passed both the Maryland and general sections on their first try. In January 1996, the Commission, by regulation, increased the number of hours of classroom instruction required for salesperson licensing from 45 to 90. This increase in instructional time was designed to prepare candidates more thoroughly and to help a greater proportion to succeed.

In 1998, the Maryland General Assembly, by statute, shortened the course to 60 hours to meet the real estate industry's need for more incoming workers.

The goal of regulation, as of any exercise of the police power of the state, is **protection of the public interest**. *The public interest* refers not only to consumers but also to the business community. The length of today's educational requirement is a compromise designed to meet the needs of both constituencies.

THE REAL ESTATE LICENSE EXAMINATION

Psychological Services, Inc. (PSI), of Glendale, California, an independent testing service under contract with the Commission, prepares and administers the prelicensing examination. PSI's testing program is adapted to each state's real estate license laws and practices and to the priorities of its licensing agency.

Candidates for broker or salesperson licenses must meet the required educational requirements before taking their examination.

PSI reports two scores for every examination: the state section score and the general section score. The passing grade set by the Commission is currently 75 percent. One must achieve at least that score on both sections to qualify for licensure.

The **general section** of the examination contains 80 questions based on general real estate information. Subjects include Property Ownership, Laws of Agency, Contracts, Real Estate Mathematics, Valuation and Real Estate Economics, Financing, Land Use Controls and Regulations, and Specialty Areas.

The **state-specific section** examination contains questions on the Brokers Act and related Maryland laws and regulations. There are 30 state-specific questions on the salesperson examination and 40 on the broker examination. These questions deal with Duties and Powers of the Commission, including the Guaranty Fund; Licensing, including Continuing Education Requirements; and Business Conduct, including Fair Housing Laws. Each of these subjects is discussed in this volume.

Because they are not pre-printed but are generated daily from a computer database, the examinations can be continually updated and revised.

APPLICATION PROCEDURES

Students may obtain the **Candidate Guide** containing instructions and application forms from the institution where they fulfill their educational requirements. Those wishing to take the examination should mail the application form to the address shown on that form together with the registration fee. Failure to follow the instructions on the registration form may result in students' not being scheduled promptly for the examinations they request.

The registration fee for taking the Maryland Real Estate Licensing Examination (either broker or salesperson) is $46. Payment can be made to PSI by check, money order, company check or cashier's check.

Candidates who have previously provided certification of examination eligibility to PSI can register with PSI by mail or through *Express Registration*. Express Registration, which may be done by phone or FAX, using a valid VISA or MasterCard, costs an additional $10—a total of $56.

After applicants have sent their applications and the necessary documents directly to PSI, PSI contacts them to schedule their examination.

By calling 1-800-733-9267, three days or more before their scheduled testing date, registered candidates may request a change in their appointment. All examinations, however, must be taken within 90 days of registration, or the candidates must repeat the process and pay another registration fee.

The registration form asks for information needed by the Commission to process the license application. It also asks for certification that the candidate has successfully completed the mandatory educational hours and a statement of irrevocable consent, which applies to out-of-state applicants.

Applicants must answer the application questions to the best of their ability. The form is signed as an affidavit, subject to the penalties of perjury.

TESTING PROCEDURES

Candidates may take an examination at any of the four testing centers located in Baltimore, Salisbury, College Park and Hagerstown. All candidates must bring positive identification to the testing site.

PSI uses a computerized testing system approved by the Commission. Upon conclusion of the testing session, the computer will inform candidates whether they passed or failed; official notification of examination results, however, will be mailed to candidates. The computerized real estate examinations are administered every business day during the week at most locations. There is no "walk in" registration.

Candidates take their examinations seated at specially designed computer work stations. On-screen instructions provide a 15- to 20-minute tutorial in the use of the keyboard. Only eight keys are used. Taking the test requires no computer skills. Instructions appear on the screen to guide the candidate through each step of the test. The testing period is 120 minutes. There is a clock for the candidate to watch.

When candidates first take the real estate exam, they answer intermixed general and state-specific questions. Candidates who have already taken the exam but only passed one of its two sections are permitted to retake the group of questions—state or general—they still need to pass. Candidates must pass both sets of questions to be eligible for a Maryland real estate license.

TYPES OF QUESTIONS ON THE EXAM

The multiple-choice answer format is used. An incomplete statement or a question is presented and is followed by four possible answers. Applicants are sometimes asked to **find the one correct answer**. At other times they must find the **one wrong answer**. Here are examples of each:

Example 1

Which one of the following agreements is most likely to be valid?

a. Owners orally agree to take their house off the market as a result of an expected offer from a potential buyer, whose spouse has not seen the house.

b. Owners of a large house in a university town agree to rent a room to a 17-year-old college student for $450 per month.

c. Owners have a signed agreement to sell their house in return for a down payment plus monthly payments over a 15-year period.

d. Owners agree to rent their house to a coach for $750 for two days, to hold a beer keg party for the high school football team.

Example 2.

A Maryland real estate licensee may take all of the following kinds of listing agreement EXCEPT one that

a. allows the sellers also to list their home with other brokers.

b. allows the broker to keep all sales proceeds in excess of a stated amount.

c. allows the sellers to find their own buyers and avoid paying the stated commission.

d. allows the broker to collect a commission regardless of who sells the property during the period of the listing.

The PSI testing approach is designed to test reasoning processes as well as factual real estate knowledge. In the examination there are questions on general real estate information, the Brokers Act and COMAR, as well as math problems and several kinds of comprehensive problems. Examples of such questions and problems have been included in most chapters of this volume so that you will become familiar with them and be better prepared for the examination.

In answering these types of questions, consider each answer carefully and eliminate the least likely ones instead of randomly selecting an answer. However, it is better to guess than to give no answer at all. The purpose of the examination is to provide a measure of your knowledge of real estate and thereby allow you to demonstrate your qualification for licensure. You should try to answer all questions without spending too much time on any one question.

Here are the answers to the model questions:

1. a   b   c   d
   [ ]   [ ]   [x]   [ ]

2. a   b   c   d
   [ ]   [x]   [ ]   [ ]

Applicants may use calculators without a keyboard containing the alphabet for the broker and salesperson license examinations. They may use PSI-provided scratch paper at the computer testing table. The fourth answer/choice to each math test item is typically "none of the above." Do not be surprised by it.

MORE HELP IN PREPARING FOR THE LICENSE EXAMINATION

We have tried to prepare you for the Maryland Real Estate License Examination by including in this volume the kinds of items usually found on the test. Familiarity with the test items in this book, however, will not in itself ensure a passing score. Your most important preparation for this examination involves thoughtfully studying real estate principles and practices.

Concentrate on learning the material by studying the text and this supplement. When using the tests and exercises in these books, be sure that you find and understand the correct solutions for any questions you miss. Use the answer key in the back of this book thoughtfully.

Real Estate Education Company® publishes other instructional materials in addition to *Modern Real Estate Practice* and *Maryland Real Estate: Practice and Law,* specially designed to aid you in passing the licensing exam: *Mastering Real Estate Mathematics,* Sixth Edition, by Ventolo, Tamper and Allaway; *Study Guide for Modern Real Estate Practice,* by Lank; and *Guide to Passing the PSI Real Estate Exam, Third Edition,* by Sager. If copies of these books are not available through your local bookseller, you may purchase them directly from the publisher, using the order form at the back of this book.

Practice with the **interactive software** for the Sager book will give you the experience of answering on-screen questions similar to state exam questions while seated at a computer keyboard—the way you will take your test.

The most effective way to **master** the basics for the general exam in to use the *Success Master Software*, version 2.0. Although it is not designed to teach test-taking, its thousands of questions, multiple-choice, yes-or-no, true-or-false and fill-in-the blanks, are designed to build **fluency and mastery** in the use of all basic real estate terminology and concepts. Such fluency and mastery are the heart of successful test taking.

TYPICAL MARYLAND–SPECIFIC TEST ITEMS

The Maryland-related questions throughout this volume are similar to those found on the real estate licensing exam. Use them to identify strengths and weaknesses in your knowledge. List the items you miss and use that list as a guide to further intensive study of the text. Sometimes you may want to test yourself on an entire list of questions. Other times you may wish to attempt the items one by one, checking your answers as you go. Decide why every correct answer IS correct. In items that ask you to find the WRONG answer, do so; but then try to learn all you can from the three CORRECT answers to the same questions. Make intelligent use of all practice questions and the answer keys.

PRACTICE QUESTIONS

1. When unlicensed salespersons negotiate a sale of real property, the commission is payable to

   a. the broker only.
   b. no one.
   c. the salesperson only.
   d. the broker and the salesperson.

2. If a salesperson license is issued on September 20, 1999, it will expire

   a. on September 20, 2001.
   b. on September 20, 2000.
   c. on April 30, 2000.
   d. on April 30, 2002.

3. When prospective purchasers first arrive at a brokerage office, what is their status under the Brokers' Act?

   a. Customers
   b. Clients
   c. Agents
   d. Factors

4. Salespersons' licenses must be

   a. kept in a safe place by the salespersons.
   b. carried by the salespersons.
   c. displayed in their brokers' offices.
   d. maintained in their personnel files by their brokers.

5. The maximum amount that a claimant may collect per claim from the Guaranty Fund is

   a. unlimited.   c. $25,000.
   b. $250,000.   d. $10,000.

6. When the license of a broker is suspended or revoked, the broker's salespeople must

   a. find a new employer.
   b. continue listing and selling.
   c. stop listing and selling.
   d. obtain a broker's license.

7. Membership on the State Real Estate Commission includes

   a. licensed salespersons only.
   b. licensed brokers only.
   c. unlicensed persons and licensed brokers and salespersons.
   d. those persons appointed by the Attorney General.

8. Licenses are issued

   a. by the Real Estate Board.
   b. to all applicants who have successfully passed required educational courses.
   c. to all brokers who have successfully passed required education courses.
   d. by the Real Estate Commission.

9. When a broker provides brokerage services through a partnership, which of the following statements is FALSE?

   a. The broker is responsible for the real estate brokerage activities of the partnership.
   b. The broker must have a contractual or employment agreement with the partnership.
   c. The broker must be one of the partners.
   d. The broker must be designated by the partnership as its broker of record.

10. If builders sell houses they have built and own, which of the following is TRUE?

   a. They need not hold real estate licenses.
   b. They must be licensed if they sell more than 6 houses in a calendar year.
   c. They must be licensed brokers.
   d. They may be licensed as salespersons and not affiliated with brokers.

11. Ethical standards that must be observed by all real estate licensees are set by the

   a. National Association of REALTORS®
   b. State Real Estate Commission.
   c. Maryland Association of REALTORS®
   d. local Boards or Associations.

12. A developer desiring to convert a building that is more than five years old into a time-share project in Maryland must

    a. give each tenant 180 days' notice.
    b. give each tenant 120 days' notice.
    c. not give tenants any prior notice.
    d. notify each tenant within 10 days after filing the Public Offering Statement.

13. The responsibilities of real estate licensees do NOT include

    a. fair treatment of third parties.
    b. competence in performance of duties.
    c. duty to give legal interpretations.
    d. loyalty to their principal.

14. In what states do lenders receive defeasible fee interests in mortgaged land?

    a. Title theory states
    b. Lien theory states
    c. Modified lien theory states
    d. Trust theory states

15. Under the Maryland Real Estate Brokers Act, the Commission may impose a penalty per violation. The penalty is

    a. $500 and/or one year in jail.
    b. $5,000.
    c. up to $2,000.
    d. up to $1,000 and/or one year in jail.

16. The amount of commission set in a listing agreement is determined by

    a. state law.
    b. the local Board or Association of REALTORS®.
    c. mutual agreement.
    d. the Real Estate Commission.

17. Earnest money received by salespersons must be

    a. deposited in their trust accounts.
    b. given to the sellers of the property.
    c. placed in their broker's safe.
    d. given to their broker for deposit in the firm's trust account.

18. Which of the following is NOT true about tenancy by the entirety?

    a. If husband and wife divorce, it is terminated.
    b. Both spouses' signatures are required to sell such property during both spouses' lifetimes.
    c. Upon death of either spouse, it converts to tenancy in common.
    d. In Maryland, only a legally married husband and wife can own property under it.

19. When a broker receives a less-than-full-price offer from a prospect and at the same time a full-price offer through a cooperating firm, the broker should present

    a. only the full price offer.
    b. only the offer from the broker's customer.
    c. both offers.
    d. the first offer received and if it is rejected, present the other offer.

20. The Maryland law requiring certain contracts to be in writing in order to be enforceable is called the

    a. written instrument law.
    b. parol evidence law.
    c. statute of limitations.
    d. statute of frauds.

Answer Key

These answers are given for each chapter in order to help you make maximum use of the tests. If you did not answer a question correctly, **restudy the course material until you understand the correct answer.**

Part I	Chapter 4/5	Chapter 7	Chapter 10	Chapter 14/15	Practice Items
1. c	1. b	1. c	1. d	1. b	1. b
2. b	2. a	2. b	2. c	2. d	2. a
3. d	3. c	3. c	3. c	3. a	3. b
4. a	4. d	4. a	4. d	4. b	4. c
5. b	5. a	5. d	5. c	5. c	5. c
6. c	6. b	6. a		6. a	6. c
7. c	7. d				7. c
8. b	8. c		**Chapter 11**		8. d
9. c	9. d	**Chapter 8**		**Chapter 16**	9. c
10. c	10. a		1. a		10. a
11. d	11. d	1. b	2. b	1. b	11. b
12. d	12. c	2. c	3. a	2. a	12. b
13. b	13. d	3. b	4. d	3. a	13. c
14. b	14. b	4. a	5. b	4. b	14. a
15. b	15. b	5. b		5. b	15. c
16. c		6. c		6. b	16. c
17. c		7. a	**Chapter 12**	7. a	17. d
18. a	**Chapter 6**	8. b		8. b	18. c
19. b		9. b	1. c	9. d	19. c
20. b		10. d	2. d	10. a	20. d
21. a	1. a	11. c	3. d		
22. d	2. c	12. d	4. c		
23. b	3. b	13. a		**Chapter 20**	
24. a	4. b				
25. a	5. a			1. d	
26. b	6. c	**Chapter 9**	**Chapter 13**	2. a	
27. a	7. c			3. b	
28. b	8. d	1. a	1. d	4. a	
	9. d	2. b	2. b		
	10. a	3. c	3. a		
		4. d	4. c		
		5. c			

Index